Haviland Collectables & Objects of Art

by
Mary Frank Gaston

Haviland Collectables
& Objects of Art

by
Mary Frank Gaston

COLLECTOR BOOKS

A Division of Schroeder Publishing Co., Inc.

The current values in this book should be used only as a guide. They are not intended to set prices, which vary from one section of the country to another. Auction prices as well as dealer prices vary greatly and are affected by condition as well as demand. Neither the Author nor the Publisher assumes responsibility for any losses that might be incurred as a result of consulting this guide.

Other books by Mary Frank Gaston:
  The Collector's Encyclopedia of Limoges Porcelain
  The Collector's Encyclopedia of R.S. Prussia
  Blue Willow
  The Collector's Encyclopedia of Flow Blue China

Additional copies of this book may be ordered from:

COLLECTOR BOOKS
P.O. Box 3009
Paducah, Kentucky 42001

or

Mary Frank Gaston
P.O. Box 342
Bryan, Texas 77806

@$19.95 Add $1.00 for postage and handling.

Copyright: Mary Frank Gaston, 1984
ISBN: 0-89145-252-4

Printed by IMAGE GRAPHICS, Paducah, Kentucky

Dedication

To Audrey and Dan Shanahan

Acknowledgements

For the preparation of this book, I am very grateful to Audrey and Dan Shanahan of Southern California. It is through their efforts that I was encouraged to initiate the work for this book on Haviland. The Shanahans are avid Haviland collectors and provided an extensive collection to be photographed and featured in this book. Through their own research they were also able to furnish much valuable information about the Haviland companies. Their own study of Haviland has taken them to France and Limoges, and includes personal discussions with Jean d'Albis, historian of the Haviland Company. They have been most cooperative in sharing their knowledge and providing necessary materials in the way of catalogs and marks plus reading a first draft of the manuscript. Audrey also took many of the photographs. It is indeed an understatement for me to say that this book would not have been possible without the support of Audrey and Dan Shanahan, and I am pleased to dedicate it to them.

In addition to the Shanahans' collection, Martha Schow and Steven Wheeler of Houston permitted me access to their pieces. Martha Schow operates a Haviland matching service in Houston. I sincerely appreciate her help in this project.

My husband, Jerry, photographed the majority of pieces presented in this book. He also edited the manuscript and helped design the book. I am indeed fortunate that he admires porcelain as much as I do. He is always eager to help in any and all ways to make an idea for a book a reality.

I also thank my publisher, Bill Schroeder, Collector Books, for publishing all of the photographs in color. This color presentation is a key factor in illustrating the beauty of Haviland china.

The Haviland featured in the cover photograph is courtesy of the Shanahan Collection.

Preface

Shortly after entering the antique business some years ago, I became attracted to the porcelain products made and decorated at Limoges, France. At first, I specialized in sets of porcelain dinnerware, both European and American. So I had the opportunity to come into contact with many lovely examples from France. When I became more involved in antique and collectable porcelain, I began to focus on other porcelain items, rather than primarily dinnerware. Increasingly, I leaned more and more toward pieces made in Limoges. This interest eventually led to my book, *The Collector's Encyclopedia of Limoges Porcelain* (1980).

The primary purpose of my first book on Limoges porcelain was to document the history and manufacturers of the porcelain industry whose beginnings originated in the late 1700's. I also wanted to draw attention to the fact that, contrary to extensive public notions, a very large number of companies were located at Limoges during the peak years of the industry--about 1870 to 1930--and that the Haviland Company was only one of the factories producing the fine products during that time. Although the Haviland Company ultimately became the largest and most famous of the Limoges potteries, it was by no means the first. I reminded readers that the basic difference between Haviland porcelain and that of the other Limoges companies was not quality, but rather an emphasis on certain types of items manufactured and their decoration. For example, when the word "Haviland" is mentioned, the image immediately brought to mind for most persons is tableware. But, when the word "Limoges" is mentioned, the image is art objects and decorative accessories. Not only does "Haviland" suggest tableware, but also it suggests unique decoration of delicately-colored floral transfer patterns. On much of the other "Limoges" the decoration is often handpainted rather than transfer applied, and is not limited to floral themes. The range of decoration includes fruit, portrait, animal, and scenic themes. Additionally, Limoges tableware or accessories that are transfer decorated, often have patterns more bold and brightly colored than the Haviland patterns. I stressed that there is, of course, overlapping in both decoration and types of items. But from the amount of examples available today, it is evident that Haviland produced more tableware for export than the other Limoges companies. Likewise, it is evident that other Limoges companies produced more export items termed decorative accessories or art objects (such as vases, jardinieres, cache pots, dresser items, humidors, and wall plaques, to name a few).

Because Haviland exported so much porcelain to the United States, and because (except for breakage) porcelain is virtually ageless, it is not surprising that most collectors are attempting to add pieces of a specific pattern to a set of tableware. Many sets, of course, are family heirlooms, and most were not complete when inherited. It is indeed possible to find replacements today because of the volume and variety of sets exported. For example, estimates on the number of patterns and variations of patterns vary from 20,000 to 60,000. If one takes the smaller figure and multiplies it by the pieces in just one set made from the pattern--usually close to 100 pieces--it is easy to see that with such a large production over a relatively long time period, many pieces are still available.

Haviland matching services have sprung up across the United States to match customers and pieces. Frequently, I get inquiries about the location of Limoges matching services for tableware of the other companies. To date, however, I am not able to recommend any one specializing only in non-Haviland Limoges, but I suggest Haviland matching services for they are the ones most likely to come in contact with other Limoges tableware. And, indeed, most do have pieces of other Limoges companies. This only reflects the fact that the other companies did not manufacture tableware in such vast amounts as the Haviland companies. Shops and shows throughout the United States, however, will verify the relative abundance of different items made by the other companies.

When I was researching and photographing material for my first book on Limoges, I became interested when I saw what were "exceptions" to the popular Haviland image (dainty floral patterned tableware). Each time it would occur to me that many people might not recognize this particular piece as a Haviland product. Indeed, my thoughts were confirmed by dealers who told me that when they have such Haviland examples, most people are surprised to find out that the piece was made by Haviland. Needless to say, the lack of knowledge has accounted for wonderful purchases being missed by many and saved for others who were aware and later walked away proudly with their "find."

Such information influenced me to write this book. I think that it is important for the collecting public to be aware of Haviland products which are distinguished from the popular "Haviland" image by type of object and decoration. Art objects and tableware ornately fashioned and richly decorated as well as unique non-tableware items were made by the Haviland companies.

Moreover, it is also equally important for collectors to see Haviland tableware in terms other than just "patterns" or "blanks." These are important and vital for matching a set, of course. However, collecting Haviland should not be limited to matching or completing a set. The age, the particular piece, and the beauty of the decoration of Haviland tableware--even in the "Haviland" image--make such items highly collectable on their own.

I want to emphasize that not everything with a "Haviland" name is included in this book. When collectors speak of "Haviland" they are referring to the company founded in Limoges, France, by David Haviland and carried on by his direct descendants. The firm of Theodore Haviland is included, but other porcelains carrying a Haviland name are excluded. Charles Field Haviland's company and that of his grandson, Robert Haviland, are considered to be "other" Limoges companies. They are discussed in my book, *The Collector's Encyclopedia of Limoges Porcelain*.

Another European porcelain manufacturer was Jean Haviland, one of David's grandsons. However, his porcelain company was not located in Limoges, but founded in Bavaria in 1907. He used either Jean, John, or Johann Haviland in his marks. These were not connected with either Haviland & Co. or the Theordore Haviland Company.

Also Haviland collectors do not include products from the American Theodore Haviland Company. Although this company was in fact founded by a direct descendant of David Haviland, the products were made and decorated in America, not in France. Such items should never cause confusion with the French ware because they are clearly marked "Theodore Haviland, New York" or "Theodore Haviland, Made in America," or "USA."

The first purpose of this book is to enable collectors to increase their knowledge and appreciation of the Haviland Company by taking a good look at its history. The second purpose is to show the desirability and collectability of Haviland products. Haviland porcelain, faience, and stoneware from the late 19th century and early 20th century have advantages for collecting over many other categories of antiques. The age and aesthetic qualities of Haviland products combine to create an opportunity to whet the appetite of the most devoted collector.

Mary Frank Gaston
P.O. Box 342
Bryan, Texas 77806

Please include a self-address, stamped envelope if a reply is requested.

Contents

Origins of the Haviland Company

The early history of the Haviland porcelain company in Limoges, France, is of great interest although most writing on the subject is not extensive. And most versions are over-simplified. The founding of the company, its peak of success, and later decline are reflected through the history of the entire Limoges porcelain industry. And that industry was interwoven with world conditions during a time period of about one hundred years--roughly from the late 1830s to the late 1930s.

By the beginning of the late 1830s, the superiority of porcelain over earthenware had been known for over two hundred years in the Western world. Since the early 1600s, when the Portuguese first imported such translucent ware from China, porcelain was coveted, especially by the royalty of Western Europe who imported vast amounts. Owning porcelain was a matter of prestige among the wealthy population. Europeans were not able to copy successfully the Oriental porcelain, however, although monarchs were anxious to find out how such wares could be made in their own countries; and they financed attempts to experiment in porcelain making. In Italy and France, manufacturing soft paste porcelain was successful. Many fine examples resulted, but soft paste porcelain was artificial, and was not true hard paste porcelain as the Oriental ware. Soft paste simply did not measure up to the qualities of true porcelain.

True porcelain has several qualities which make it superior to other forms of pottery. It is translucent which imparts a unique appearance. Porcelain is light weight and delicate, but it is strong and durable also. Most importantly, porcelain is vitreous. The glaze cannot be penetrated, and thus, as glass, the piece is impervious to liquids.

In contrast, earthenware is not translucent; and it chips and breaks easily. Earthenware is not completely vitreous although it may be glazed and have a vitreous look. Consequently, the glaze may become crazed which allows material to seep to the body of the object and become trapped. In addition to being unattractive, the crazed glaze is also unhealthy for tableware items. In the early days, the glaze on earthenware dishes also contained lead, which today we know is not healthy for tableware. The glaze on porcelain, however, did not contain lead. Thus, as a medium for tableware, porcelain was indeed superior to earthenware.

True porcelain was not manufactured in Europe until about 1708 when the method was discovered by Bottger of Meissen. The secret and technique of making porcelain was closely guarded by the Royal Porcelain Company of Meissen for some years. Eventually though, other centers in Europe gained this knowledge and hard paste porcelain production began in various regions and countries where the necessary ingredients were found. The primary material needed for hard paste porcelain is kaolin which occurs naturally from the decomposition of granite. This type of earth is available in only a few places in the world. It is not a common potter's clay. Thus the existence of this ingredient in a particular location largely determined where true porcelain could be made. Once this material was found and the technique known for manufacturing, experiments in hard paste porcelain could be implemented. Where this was possible, the process was still usually under royal patronage. The products that resulted were expensive and limited to the very wealthy.

The Limoges porcelain industry dates from about 1770, shortly after kaolin was discovered in the area. The industry did not develop on a large scale, however, until the first quarter of the 19th century. It was only after the French Revolution that royal monopolies were removed which allowed more factories to be founded. The number of people in the Limoges porcelain industry increased from 200 workers in 1807 to 1,800 workers in 1830 (*Revue des Industries d'art Offrir*, 1978, p. 91).

In spite of the great interest in French porcelain generally, and Haviland porcelain specifically, only a few books about the Haviland company have been written by American authors (see bibliography). Short summaries about the origins of the company are included in general books on antiques. Reference books on porcelain marks note the beginning dates of the firm and show marks used during certain time periods. Until recently, the situation was similar in France. Most historical studies focused on 18th century porcelain. The material on the late 19th century, which included Haviland, was brief and scattered or combined with other information concerning the history of the entire Limoges porcelain industry. As a consequence of scattered and inconsistent information, it is easy to understand why collectors and dealers are sometimes confused and misled about the origins and the age of Haviland pieces. It is desirable, therefore, to clarify some erroneous notions in order to provide a better understanding of Haviland.

From research leading to my first book (*The Collector's Encyclopedia of Limoges Porcelain*, 1980) on Limoges porcelain (some of which necessarily involved Haviland), and especially from a French book also published in 1980, *La Porcelain de Limoges* by Jean d'Albis and Céleste Romanet, we now have a much clearer picture of the issues which to that point have caused much confusion. Jean d'Albis is the historian of the Haviland Company (and a descendant of the Haviland family). That book, in French, covers the entire Limoges porcelain industry from its beginnings to the present, and, of course, includes several pages devoted to the Havilands.

From comparing all available material, I found three major problem areas: (1) why the Haviland Company was founded in Limoges; (2) early Haviland activities in Limoges; and (3) when Haviland actually began producing porcelain.

Haviland Moves to Limoges

Most histories about the Haviland Company relate a charming story of how a customer came into the Haviland China Shop in New York City one day (probably in 1839) trying to find a cup that matched one she had. David Haviland could not match the piece, but he knew the cup was French porcelain although the example was unmarked. He was so impressed with this cup that he immediately decided he wanted to find the manufacturer. Therefore he set out for France, where he did in fact find the company which had made the piece. He became so enamoured with French porcelain, that he brought back other tableware items to sell in New York. However, his customers were not as impressed as he was with the French items. Nonplussed, David Haviland was so convinced that French porcelain tableware was desirable, that he moved his family to France, settled in Limoges, and began producing porcelain tableware which he exported to the United States. His business venture was an immediate success from the beginning!

This story fits all of the clichés of the "American dream" or "overnight success." We enjoy hearing about these types of business ventures where riches apparently result quickly from luck or chance. On close inspection and reflection, however, this story seems a bit too easy when taken at face value. One wonders if there is not more to the story? Would a New York businessman, upon seeing a particular piece of china that he did not have, be so impetuous that he would immediately set off for France--a very long trip-- to find its source and obtain a match for his customer? Upon his return, finding that the other examples of French porcelain which he brought back did not sell well, would he still decide to uproot his family and move to France to make such products to be sold, not in France, but in America? This seems a very risky and impractical thing to

do. Why was David Haviland so convinced that the American public would change its mind about the French tableware? The answer and underlying basis for the foundation of the Haviland Company can be found in one word--"Porcelain."

In the mid to late 1830s, when David Haviland was engaged in the business of selling tableware in New York City, the European hard paste porcelain industry in France, whose products were brought primarily by the wealthy, was clearly not familiar to most Americans. And at this time, although the Haviland family was engaged in selling tableware or dishes, they were primarily earthenware imported from England. Because the American porcelain industry was only beginning to be developed, and because of America's ties with England, it was natural that English ware was the type available. England's pottery industry was concentrated on the production of earthenware rather than porcelain. But, it is clear that David Haviland knew that porcelain was a better tableware than English earthenware.

David Haviland first worked for his brother, Edmond, selling china in New York City. In 1838, he and another brother, Daniel, established a china importing business. So he had several years experience in the business of buying and selling tableware. Therefore, if he knew porcelain was better than earthenware, one could ask, "Why wasn't he selling it?" According to d'Albis and Romanet (1980, p. 133), David Haviland had in fact imported such products in order to see if they would improve his business. Because the American economy had been in a severe condition since 1836, David and his brother wanted to see if French porcelain would sell better than the English earthenware which had declined in sales.

The brothers found out after they had imported porcelain from France, however, that the American customers did not appreciate the products. Americans did not object to the pieces being made of porcelain, but they did not like the dishes themselves. The plates were too small, sets included pieces which were not used by Americans, and the ware was not decorated to their liking. Therefore, knowing the advantages of porcelain and knowing why his customers did not like the French items, David Haviland personally made a trip to France in 1840 to see how he might obtain French tableware that would be compatible to American eating habits.

This information clarifies David Haviland's interest in porcelain and the reason for his first trip to France in 1840. He did not make the trip on a whim--just to match a particular cup--but based on a business strategy. From his knowledge of the superiority of tableware made of porcelain rather than earthenware, coupled with knowing what Americans expected sets of tableware to consist of and look like, he was in a position to see how French wares could be adapted for American consumption.

What David found out during his first trip to France in 1840 must have looked promising, because he moved to France in 1841, with his wife and first child, Charles Edward. He did not immediately go to Limoges, but to Foécy. It is noted that in Foécy Haviland stayed with his friend and French supplier, Pillivuyt, who was connected with the French porcelain industry (d'Albis and Romanet, p. 133).

Early Years in Limoges

According to d'Albis and Romanet (p. 133), David Haviland actually moved on to Limoges from Foécy in 1842 and spent the first five years in Limoges choosing porcelain products made by various companies which he exported to his New York based business. In 1847 he opened his own decorating shop in Limoges. He arranged for other companies to make items according to his specifications, especially for him, which were decorated at his studio by the artists he employed. In 1853, he received permission to build his own factory for manufacturing porcelain. (I show 1853 in my first book on Limoges porcelain as the date when Haviland opened a factory, based on references available to me at that time. Clearly, that was just the date when Haviland obtained permission to construct a factory.)

The process of building a factory did not progress quickly. We find that although Haviland was able to move his studio to the new location in 1855, he still was able only to decorate porcelain made by other companies. His furnaces for porcelain production were not ready, but his mufles were (d'Albis and Romanet, p. 134). This enabled him to decorate but not to produce porcelain. Decorated porcelain had to be fired in mufles, a small oven, before the decorating process was complete in order to set or "fix" the decoration. The temperature in these ovens was high, but much lower than furnace temperatures which were required to fire the paste that would result in true porcelain.

Haviland's First Production in Limoges

Several references cite or imply the early 1840s as the beginning date of the Haviland Company in Limoges. My research on the subject discovered that was not the date French chronicles identified. Although they, like the American references, noted that David Haviland settled in Limoges in 1842, French sources did not say that he started producing porcelain from that year. At first, he was known to have decorated the whiteware made by other Limoges companies. Although American authors also indicate that David Haviland first decorated the porcelain made by other companies, they do not say precisely when he actually began producing porcelain. Instead, either they skirt the issue or they ignore the question entirely. Thus readers infer that production began during the early 1840s.

According to d'Albis and Romanet (p. 134), the year, 1865, marks the time when porcelain was first manufactured at the Haviland company in Limoges, France. We see that there was quite a time span, a period of 23 years, from when David Haviland first settled in Limoges (1842) and when the first porcelain was issued from his factory. If one thinks about it, one should realize that manufactur-

ing porcelain, especially at that time in history, was a complicated process. One could not just arrive in Limoges and immediately began producing porcelain, even if one had knowledge of selling tableware.

During those twenty-three years, David Haviland learned the business. While he was purchasing, designing, and decorating stock from other companies, he was becoming knowledgeable of the factors necessary for setting up his own company to manufacture porcelain. Based on the success of the products he exported to America during this time, he knew that his expansion into the manufacturing end of the industry was warranted. Also during this era, he was establishing a name for himself in the Limoges industry with his designs and decorations. It was during the 1850s that objects designed and decorated by the Haviland studio won medals at Exhibitions: in London in 1851, in New York in 1853, and in Paris in 1855. Large vases, urns, and elaborate tableware items were exhibited.

This is a very noteworthy and important part of the Haviland history. Porcelain exists as a medium for artistic expression in shapes and decoration. Haviland designed the shapes and commissioned other factories to make up the shapes in porcelain which were then decorated by his artists. However, when we are erroneously informed that Haviland porcelain originated in 1842 and are not told that the year is merely the date of his moving to Limoges, we are surely going to think that the Haviland factory and products later manufactured by Haviland are older than they are; moreover, it diminishes the role of the other potters connected with the Limoges porcelain industry. Needless to say, if these other companies had not been in existence before and during this period of the Haviland Company, he would not have been able to supply or decorate tableware for American consumption.

This fact should not detract from the importance of the Haviland firm, but should allow us to understand and to appreciate more fully the significance of the entire Limoges porcelain industry in general as well as to understand Haviland's important role in that industry. Those beginnings laid the foundation for the ultimate success of his company: Haviland became not only the most famous Limoges porcelain manufacturer in the eyes of America, but in the eyes of the rest of the world, and especially within the Limoges porcelain industry.

The products of the Haviland Company occupy a unique place in the history of this country. Many people are aware of the name "Haviland" even if they do not own any Haviland porcelain, or if they are not interested in antiques. Some of these people may never try to find out the history of the company, and others may rely on information they are given by those who do. Persons who seek and eventually relate information will only be able to know and tell what they have read. It is important, therefore, to be factual if we can concerning dates not only for the sake of history, but also to be able to place Haviland products in their proper chronology because such dates are a vital part of the Haviland history.

In summary, although Haviland did not produce porcelain until 1865, his design and decoration of French Limoges porcelain earned him a reputation in the world well before that time. Also there is no question that David Haviland was definitely the key to opening up the export market for Limoges porcelain to America as well as other parts of the world. From statistics of Limoges porcelain exported, it is a fact that he was indeed the largest exporter even during the time before he manufactured his own porcelain.

David Haviland possessed the ultimate talents of a businesman. He was able to know what the public wanted before they knew they wanted it. He was able to provide the products for them when they discovered that they wanted and must have such products. With this overview, let us turn now to the further development and chronology of the Haviland Companies.

Chronology of the Haviland Companies

The several names or titles under which the Haviland Company has operated reflect its chronology. The development and progress of the firm can also be traced through events that occurred during these specific periods when the business was conducted under various names.

When David Haviland settled in Limoges in 1842 and started exporting porcelain to the United States, he was doing business under the firm name of "D. G. and D. Haviland" (Daniel Griffin and David), the name of his New York based china importing company, formed in 1838 with his brother Daniel. In 1852, that company name was changed to "Haviland Bros. & Co." when another brother, Robert, joined the firm. Thus, the business operations in Limoges under David were also changed similarly. The Limoges end of the family business continued under that title until 1863.

In 1863, David Haviland severed his connections with the New York company. The firm in New York was having business difficulties and had to close in 1865. Its downfall was caused in large part by the American Civil War (d'Albis and Romanet, p. 134).

After breaking off his association with Haviland Bros. in New York, David formed his own company in 1864 with his sons, Charles Edward and Theodore under the title of "Haviland & Cie." (Cie. is the French abbreviation for *Compagnie*). The company operated under that title for a relatively long period: 1864 to 1930. However, several developments during that time brought changes in the management and ownership.

Soon after "Haviland & Cie." (or in English, "Haviland & Co.") was formed in 1864, the nature of the business changed from solely designing and decorating porcelain to manufacturing (1865) as well. Earlier I noted that it took twenty three years for David Haviland to be able to take part in the manufacturing end of the industry. Once the company did begin manufacturing its own porcelain, however, its progress and expansion were swift. David's sons were the really active leaders of the company after 1865. Charles was in charge of managing the factory in Limoges, and Theodore went to New York to be in charge of the importing affairs for the company. Business did not cease with America during this period, even though the old "Haviland Bros." was out of business. Theodore was able to set up his own distribution center for the porcelain

products. Meanwhile, back in Limoges, new techniques in production and decorating were instituted, and the size of the factory was expanded shortly after 1865. According to d'Albis and Romanet (p. 136) the company's products were so successful in America during this time that Haviland still found it necessary to have part of his porcelain made by other companies in Limoges. The authors note that this was also a way of obtaining a partial monopoly of the American market.

In the early 1870s, Charles Haviland also decided to experiment in other forms of pottery making besides porcelain. His interest in the arts and acquaintance with the leading Parisian artists at that time were instrumental in causing this new venture. A new wave was taking place in the art world which sought to interpret subjects in a natural rather than a classical manner. "Naturalism" and "Impressionism" were the terms for this form of artistic expression. Charles Haviland decided to establish a studio in Paris for experimenting with works made of earthenware as a dimension of this new art form.

The first studio was located in the Auteuil district of Paris. Felix Bracquemond, head of the Sèvres decorating factory, was persuaded to take over the direction of the studio. He hired artists schooled in this new art form to design and decorate the art pottery. These products were made of an earthenware base, "terra cotta," with a metallic glaze, which was thus a form of "faience." According to Simodynes and Simodynes (1983a), this medium allowed decoration to be hand painted on the surface, with the result that it had the appearance of an oil painting. "Barbotine" was the term used to describe this particular form of handpainted decoration.

Vases and jardinieres were the primary objects made by the Auteuil studio. These were often large with decoration in relief. Floral designs appear to have been the primary decoration theme, but other outdoor subjects and people can also be seen on examples (see pp. 22-23). Other pieces were decorated in a style showing the Japanese influence which was just becoming popular in Western Europe. In 1875, L'Escalier de Cristal in Paris became the exclusive outlet for the Haviland art pottery. These works made at the Auteuil studio from about 1873 to 1880 were highly praised. They were especially noted at the Philadelphia Exposition in 1876. The examples exhibited became a direct influence on the works of American potters during the late 1800s.

Bracquemond left the Auteuil studio in 1881, and the production of faience was discontinued about 1882. At that time the studio moved to a new location on Blomet Street. The work there was under the direction of Ernest Chaplet, a noted scientist in the pottery field. He had in fact invented the "Barbotine" technique. Under his direction, the pottery medium was changed from faience to stoneware with some additional work with porcelain bodies (Simodynes and Simodynes, 1983b).

Although the art pottery and stoneware were artistically successful, they were not commercially successful. After a few years, the demand did not warrant the production costs, and this facet of the Paris business was discontinued in 1886. However, the studio still remained open to design decoration for the Haviland porcelain factory at Limoges until 1914 (Jacobson, 1979, p. 138).

David Haviland died in 1879. The business was continued with Charles Edward and Theodore as partners. Theodore returned to France from New York and became involved with the business in Limoges. The production continued to flourish. Eventually, though, Theodore became dissatisfied because he did not have as much control and power in the company as he desired. As a result the company was dissolved in 1891. According to d'Albis and Romanet (p. 139), Charles Edward immediately reorganized in 1892 under the same name of "Haviland & Co." His eldest son, George, became his partner. Theodore formed his own company also in 1892 under the name of "Theodore Haviland."

The "new" or "second" "Haviland & Co." continued to prosper after the brothers separated, and the Theodore Haviland Company did not take long in getting its share of the market. Theodore's factory was ready in 1893. It had the newest equipment and employed large numbers of workers in all phases of manufacturing. Many new shapes and patterns were introduced, and skilled artists were employed to design the decoration for the porcelain. The company won the Grand Prize at the Paris Exhibition in 1900 (d'Albis and Romanet, p. 141).

The late 1890s through the early 1900s were a peak period not only for the Haviland companies, but for the entire Limoges porcelain industry. Local and world events, soon after the turn of the century, were beginning to take shape, however, which would lead to the industry's downfall.

Serious labor problems between the owners and workers of the porcelain factories in Limoges occurred in 1905 which disrupted the industry. In 1907, an embargo was placed on Limoges imports into the United States. American potters were concerned over such vast amounts of imported wares which they saw as unfair competition for their own products (d'Albis and Romanet, p. 141). These events were soon followed by World War I from 1914 to 1918 which caused the industy to come to a virtual standstill.

The brothers, Charles Edward and Theodore, did not live long after the first World War. Theodore died in 1919, and Charles Edward died in 1921. The oldest sons took over the respective companies: William--the Theodore Haviland Company; and George--Haviland and Co.

During the years immediately following World War I, the Limoges porcelain industry attempted to re-establish itself. Times were changing, however, from the period of the late Victorian era. Life styles and artistic tastes were in a state of transition. The ornate and floral designs popular at an earlier period were giving way to preferences for more simple styles and decoration. Porcelain tableware was of course influenced by these changes. William Haviland (d'Albis and Romanet, p. 142), met this challenge by having his artists design such pieces that would reflect this changing style. Sandoz, Jean Dufy, and Suzanne Lalique are some of the artists who worked for the Theodore Haviland Company after the first World War and during the 1920s. Their designs and artistry reflected the new "modern" style of simple line and simple decoration.

William Haviland exhibited such innovative designs at the Exposition of Decorative Arts in 1925 in Paris. He is noted to have presented five table services in different patterns reflecting the new "modern" trend (McClinton, *Art Deco: A Guide For Collectors*, 1972, pp. 108 and 109). The 1925 Exhibition in fact introduced what is now called the Art Deco period. The art form in all types of media was expressed in simple lines and geometric shapes with designs often painted in black or silver or sharply contrasting colors as opposed to the flowing and ornate designs of the previous Art Nouveau era or the earlier rococo styles. The Art Deco trend initiated in 1925 remained popular for about twenty years and has resurfaced with much enthusiasm today.

After a brief respite from war, however, other world conditions again arose which shadowed and overtook the industry. Increased porcelain imports in the American market from other European countries competed with the Limoges products. The stock market crash of 1929 in the United States followed by the Great Depression took their toll on the Limoges companies. The Haviland firms had the most to lose during that time, for they were the largest exporters.

Haviland and Company under George's management was forced to close in 1930. This, according to d'Albis and Romanet (p. 139) was caused by a business arrangement George entered in 1925. At that time he joined forces with a financial group headed by the Mirabeau bank. This group took control of the porcelain manufacturing operations in Limoges, and George went to New York to direct the American importing end of the business. Because of inflation, the firm in Limoges wanted to increase the previously agreed-upon prices that the firm was charging the New York company. George Haviland did not agree to this. As a result the Mirabeau bank closed the business in 1930 and decided to liquidate its assets. Although William Haviland made an offer for the company, because of the bad relationship between their fathers, the two cousins were not in close contact, and George did not know of his cousin's offer. As a consequence the firm of Gérard, Duffraisseix and Abbot purchased the models and marks of the company. The company founded by David Haviland was thus ended.

After Haviland and Co. was liquidated, its huge remaining stock of wares was sold at very low prices which was detrimental to the other companies. A similar occurence with the stock of the Guérin-Pouyat Company in 1933 also had a tremendous negative impact on the whole industry. Production figures for companies in Limoges greatly reflect the downward spiral: in 1931, production was only 69% of that in 1924; by 1938, production was only 20% of 1924; and by 1944, production was only 11% of the 1924 production (d'Albis and Romanet, p. 143).

In 1936, William Haviland decided to establish a porcelain factory in America in order to increase the firm's business and compensate for the continuing decline of the Limoges porcelain industry in the American market. In Limoges, conditions only worsened after this time with the outbreak of World War II in Europe. During this period, from 1939 to 1944, the industry was again virtually at a stand-still.

In 1941, William Haviland was able to obtain the rights to the old Haviland and Co. marks and models which had been sold in 1931. This action allowed the Theodore Haviland Company in France to revert once more to "Haviland" alone for the name of the company. The firm started by David Haviland was again one firm, under the name of "Haviland S.A." The company formed by William in New York continued under the name of "Theodore Haviland."

It was not an easy task for the porcelain industry in France to prosper following the war. The devastation brought about by the war necessitated rebuilding and repairs and modernization of the plants if they were to compete in the world porcelain market. The reconstruction took a long time. Life styles following the war were negative for the industry. Men and women were both working, and households did not have domestic help as some had in previous generations. Everyday living was becoming simpler, and as a result entertaining more informal. There was not the same demand for large porcelain dinner services. Brides were beginning also to choose other fine German and American porcelain or perhaps no porcelain at all. In the 1950s plastic for everyday use became desirable, and an inexpensive set of earthenware and later stoneware became the choices for a "best set" of dishes for new couples preparing to set up a household.

The Haviland Company did not fold up in light of these circumstances, however. Although the process was slow, the company under the management of William's sons implemented a modernization program which enabled the firm to get back on its feet. According to d'Albis and Romanet (p.143), William Haviland retired in 1957 with management passing to his sons, who in turn retired in 1972 turning the management of the company over to other individuals. The Haviland Company is once again esteemed in the eyes of the world as a porcelain manufacturer. The products in style, type, and decoration are quite different from those produced during the golden age of Haviland from the late 1800s to the early 1900s, however.

For a concise summary of this section, I have compiled a chronology of important milestones of the Haviland Company which follows:

1829 - David Haviland joins brother Edmond in shop in New York City selling tableware.

1838 - David Haviland forms a china importing firm with his brother, Daniel in New York City under the title of "D. G. and D. Haviland."

1838 - "D. G. & D. Haviland" first imports French
1839 porcelain.

1840 - David goes to France to see how porcelain products might be made suitable for the American market.

1841 - David moves to Foécy, France with his wife and two year old son, Charles Edward.

1842 - David moves to Limoges. His son, Theodore, is born.

1842 - David begins exporting porcelain, made by other
1847 Limoges companies, to the United States.

1847 - David establishes a decorating studio to decorate porcelain manufactured by other Limoges companies.

1852 - "D. G. & D. Haviland" changes to "Haviland Bros. & Co." when another brother, Robert, enters the business.

1853 - David obtains permission to construct a factory for manufacturing porcelain.

1855 - David moves studio to the new factory; work remains confined to designing and decorating porcelain manufactured by others.

1863 - David breaks off his association with "Haviland Bros. & Co." in New York.

1864 - David forms his own firm--"Haviland & Cie."-- in Limoges with his sons, Charles Edward and Theodore.

1865 - "Haviland and Cie." begins producing porcelain at Limoges. Charles manages Limoges factory. Theodore takes over the New York importing and distributing affairs of the company.

1872 - Under the direction of Charles, the Auteuil studio in Paris is opened for the production of art pottery.

1879 - David Haviland dies. Charles and Theodore continue the company. Theodore returns to France.

1882 - Production of faience ceases and a new studio is opened on Blomet Street in Paris for production of stoneware with Chaplet in charge.

1886 - Production of stoneware ceases at the Paris studio.

1891 - "Haviland & Cie." is dissolved.

1892 - Charles, with his son George, forms new company under the previously used title of "Haviland & Co." Theodore forms new company under the name of "Theodore Haviland."

1919 - Theodore Haviland dies, and his son, William, takes control of the "Theodore Haviland" company.

1921 - Charles Edward Haviland dies, and his son, George, takes over control of "Haviland & Co."

1925 - "Haviland & Co." is divided by George with a group headed by the Mirabeau bank, which takes charge of the Limoges business; George goes to New York to manage the importing and distributing side of the business.

1930 - "Haviland & Co." is closed.

1931 - "Haviland & Co." is liquidated.

1936 - William Haviland establishes an American company in New York also under the name of "Theodore Haviland."

1941 - William Haviland obtains the rights to marks and models of "Haviland & Co." This allows the French Theodore Haviland Company to reorganize under the name "Haviland S. A."

1957 - William Haviland retires and his sons take over "Haviland S. A." They institute modernization of the plant.

1972 - From 1972 onward, other individuals have headed "Haviland S. A."

Suggestions for Collecting Haviland

The name "Haviland" has been well known in the field of antique and collectable china for many years, but the interest in the products has largely been confined to matching patterns rather than collecting Haviland for its own sake. Today, the interest in Haviland products is broadening. The emphasis on art objects has increased and unusual pieces are highly desirable. Haviland tableware is also viewed from a different perspective.

I have divided collectable Haviland into five categories, and arranged the color photographs according to these five groups: (I) Early Haviland (prior to 1876), (II) Art Pottery, (III) Special Categories for Collectors, (IV) Decorative Accessories, and (V) Tableware and Accessories.

I. Early Haviland: Plates 1-25

The collectability of items in Category I is determined by the mark on the pieces. The marks reflect the first period of David Haviland's business in Limoges: items commissioned by Haviland and decorated by his decorating studio (1847-1865--see Marks 1-4) or porcelain made during the first period of his factory production (1865-1876--see Mark 5). Because pieces were not marked before the early 1850s, it is difficult to attribute pieces to Haviland that may have been decorated by his studio before then. Moreover, pieces were not routinely marked until 1876; thus marked specimans are rare. Such pieces are very collectable if marked. Some of those particular items are overlooked because they are utilitarian and plainly decorated. The decoration is frequently worn off, especially the gold on handles. For that reason, they are often quite reasonable in price. Exhibition pieces, however, designed and decorated by Haviland prior to 1865, or made and decorated by his company from 1865 to 1876, are also included in this category. These items are quite rare and command a premium price. Only limited examples are available for collectors because most are in museums or owned already by advanced collectors. These examples were neither mass produced, nor intended primarily for export to the United States.

II. Art Pottery: Plates 26-36

The majority of Haviland products were made of porcelain, however, the pottery and stoneware made in Paris from 1873 until 1886 are very important examples of Haviland art objects. I show some examples in the color plates, and some pictures from a catalog to illustrate the variety of the faience items manufactured during that time (see pp. 22-23). Examples were marked H & Co, H & Co, or HAVILAND & CO (see Marks 20-22). A catalog
L   Limoges
also notes that a number designating the particular shape was stamped on the base of the pieces. Some of these pieces may be artist signed: Bracquemond, Chaplet, Delapanche, Lindeneher, Midoux, Lafond, Noel, and Aube are a few of the artists who worked for the Havilands during this time. The famous French artist, Gauguin, is also noted to have been associated with the studio, however, examples of his work are extremely rare.

Although production was fairly prolific during this thirteen year period, examples of these Haviland products are relatively scarce in this country today, and prices vary. The prices seem quite reasonable, though, based on what the pieces represent. From Haviland's advertisements, it is evident that production was not intended only for export to the United States. The ads were printed in four languages --English, French, German, and Spanish.

III. Special Categories for Collectors: Plates 37-68

Porcelain items of a special nature made after 1876 (when printed marks became routine) are included in this broad category. Exhibition items, portrait pieces, busts, figures, or figurines, porcelain made for famous people or copied from the same designs, Haviland advertising pieces such as salesmen's samples, other advertising china, for particular places such as hotels or clubs, railroad china, commemorative items, and miniatures are some of the categories which have special collector interest.

Tableware items in animal form, designed by the artist Sandoz from about 1915 through the early 1920s for the Theodore Haviland Company are particularly of interest to collectors. In addition to photographs of some of these pieces, a catalog illustrating a variety of these items is found in pages 24-25. The electrical pieces featured in the same catalog by Poberejsky also reflect the new modern style of the post World War I era. Examples of those items do not seem to be available. Perhaps this is because when an electrical appliance becomes faulty, it is often discarded. This may have been the case with the Poberejsky "Bouilloires Electriques" (electric boilers).

Other porcelain manufactured by the Theodore Haviland Company during the mid 1920s reflecting the Art Deco style is also quite collectable, including, of course, pieces designed and painted by Jean Dufy and Suzanne Lalique. Pieces usually carry their signatures in addition to the company marks, but examples are extremely rare.

The prices for items in Category III vary depending on the item and the special category of collector interest. All examples are eagerly sought and command a good price. Their availability is rather scarce for limited quantities were manufactured. Additionally, in some instances collector interest is not based on the pieces being made of porcelain or made by the Haviland companies, but because of the particular collecting category it comes under--railroad china, advertising collectables, and miniatures are some examples.

IV. Decorative Accessories: Plates 69-93

Porcelain manufactured after 1876 that was designed for other purposes than eating or serving comprise this category. Vases, jardinieres, and ferners are typical examples. But ash trays, match boxes, baskets, chambersticks, dresser items, and wash sets are also examples of non-tableware manufactured by the Havilands. With some exceptions, these pieces are transfer decorated and may have matching counterparts in tableware of the same design. Large vases are quite expensive, as are complete dresser and wash sets, but smaller items are quite affordable. These types of items were not the primary production of the companies, of course, and thus they are much less commonly found. They are a quite desirable category of Haviland collecting.

V. Tableware and Accessories: Plates 94-223

A wide range of items can be found in Category V, the largest and most accessible area of collectable Haviland. Historically, most individuals' interest in Haviland tableware has been focused on completing a dinner service. As a consequence, many collectable pieces are overlooked. One reason is that people are looking for a specific pattern only and fail to see the range of possibilities for collection. Or, if people are not trying to complete a dinner service, they may fail to see or become familiar with the fact that Haviland items represent fine quality porcelain of the late 19th and early 20th centuries.

The emphasis in this category is therefore on object rather than a particular pattern or blank (the term which describes the mold or shape of an object before decoration). By looking at Haviland tableware in this manner the appeal of "Haviland" can be appreciated on a much larger scale. If one is seeking quality porcelain, handsomely decorated, dating from the late Victorian era, Haviland tableware has an outstanding and varied assortment to offer.

It is true that it is difficult, and in some cases impossible, to collect a really complete dinner service decorated with some of the old Haviland patterns or some of the most popular ones. But a lot of beautiful porcelain is sitting on the shelves of Haviland matching services and in antique shops waiting for someone who needs that particular pattern. In this day of relatively informal entertaining, and on those special occasions when we do want to set a fancy table, it is still possible to do so, and in Haviland porcelain--for pieces do not have to match. One type of pattern for a cream soup, another for a salad plate, a third for a dinner plate, accompanied by serving pieces in varied patterns combine to set an interesting and attractive table. We are not tied to the dictates of extreme rules of etiquette where everything must be matched. The prices of these pieces are really a welcome sight to the pocketbook. Just compare them with the prices of new china that is not so well made or decorated.

In addition the extra or accessory items that were made to be used with a set of dinnerware, but were optional purchases, are of collector interest because they are a specific item and thus fit into various collecting groups. Bone dishes, butter pats, ramekins, individual salts, cracker jars, and moustache cups, are examples. These types of pieces have not been available in modern services for many years.

Extra tableware services for serving coffee, tea, chocolate, punch, ice cream, berries, or pudding are highly collectable. Fish and game sets plus oyster plates are very desirable, not only for type of object, but also these often exhibit unique decoration relating to marine and outdoor life. Large platters, compotes, elegant tureens, and ornately shaped and richly decorated plates make lovely accent pieces as well as being functional.

Examples in Category V encompass a long time period--from 1876 to about 1940. Advanced collectors usually limit choices, however, to items made no later than the early 1900s. These items are primarily transfer decorated and not handpainted. Determination of approximate time of manufacture can be found by the underglaze factory mark; and whether or not it was factory decorated will be known by the presence of a second mark that is overglaze and contains the full Haviland name in most instances. As noted earlier, the H & Co mark was used overglaze in
L
various colors, but seemingly for a short period, beginning about 1878.

At present, prices for Haviland tableware and accessories are reasonable and bargains can still be found. In some instances, a particular item is unusually scarce, such as tea caddies, cracker jars, or jam jars, and prices tend to be higher for those items. A few patterns, namely, "Baltimore Rose" and "Drop Rose" are very much in demand among collectors. As a consequence, any piece in those particular patterns may command a premium price. Examples of porcelain tableware decorated with those patterns are not particularly scarce, except in certain colors other than pink or rose such as "Baltimore Rose" in gold and "Drop Rose" in white. Collector interest is responsible for the higher prices of those patterns. The pattern names are popular ones and not factory designated (see Plates 184 and 218 for an example of each). Haviland porcelain with cobalt blue decoration, in whole or in part, is also considered very desirable because of the richness of the decoration. Pieces exhibiting this color are usually higher in price than similar items with a different pattern or color.

The majority of Haviland patterns, however, are priced according to the type of item rather than by the particular pattern. This is true for even very popular patterns such as "Silver Anniversary" (popular name), "Autumn Leaf" and "Apple Blossom" (both factory names).

Further Notes on Decorating

The majority of Haviland porcelain was decorated by the transfer method of decoration. In the early days, before the mid 1870s, the outlines of the designs were transferred to the porcelain bodies and then filled in with colors by hand. When chromolithography was introduced about 1875 to the factory, the decorating process was further improved and colored designs could be transferred completely.

Transfer decoration was of course quick and less expensive than handpainting. It also allowed the cost of the decorated porcelain to be reasonable enough that the products could be purchased by more people. Most importantly, it made it possible to produce many different patterns and pattern variations. Of course enamelling and gold decoration still required individual attention, but decoration applied by transfer methods was the primary type used by both Haviland & Co. and the Theodore Haviland Company throughout their history.

Therefore when collectors refer to "factory decorated porcelain," they are speaking basically about Haviland porcelain made after 1876 which was decorated with these transfer designs. Collectors know that it is important to differentiate between "factory" decorated pieces and "non-factory" decorated pieces. The reason is because the term "factory decorated" definitely implies superior quality of decoration. This distinction is necessary because during the late Victorian period, china painting was quite popular, especially in the United States. Because of the demand for undecorated porcelain, many Limoges, including Haviland, and other European porcelain factories exported blanks during this time. Both amateur and professional artists did china painting. Many pieces decorated by amateurs show considerable artistic talent; but many pieces are poorly done. Sometimes though, the low quality of the decoration is not reflected in the price of these pieces. The price is often too high when compared to a similar item decorated at the factory. Remember, because a piece of porcelain is handpainted and even signed by an amateur artist, that does not necessarily mean that the object is desirable.

It is apparent that the Haviland companies did not export as much undecorated ware as other companies did. Examples of all types of items, however, do surface. Advanced Haviland collectors do not consider these pieces very desirable unless the whiteware object itself is unusual or the decoration is of professional quality. For example, the sardine box in Plate 201 is unusual as an object, but the decoration is obviously non-professional. Most of the blanks that were exported to this country were eventually decorated by someone; however, sometimes one comes across pieces that for some reason or another never were decorated. Such whiteware, depending on the object, often makes a very attractive addition to a collection. In fact, in some cases, we should be glad that no one ever decorated the piece! It should be noted here that one particular design of Haviland porclain has extremely high demand in its blank or undecorated state. "Ranson" was the factory name for the design or shape of these pieces (see Plate 125). It is still possible to put together a large service with serving and accessory pieces in this design. Prices for "Ranson" pieces, however, are similar to those for most Haviland patterns.

The "Ranson" design as well as other Haviland designs were decorated with gold trim and sometimes monogrammed by decorating companies in this country. Although the work is professional, unless the piece is unusual or the monogram matches one's own, collector interest is limited.

Haviland blanks not decorated at the factories are relatively easy to identify. If there is only one mark, underglaze, on the piece, it probably was not decorated at the factory. (Sometimes one may see pieces that have only one whiteware mark, but from the transfer decoration, it will be obvious that the item was decorated at the factory. Needless to say, it would have been impossible for all that porcelain to have been made without mistakes occasionally occurring in the marking process!) If the Haviland companies decorated the piece, it should have an overglaze mark as well containing one of the Haviland names. One should be aware, however, that another Haviland name may be encountered. Frank Haviland, youngest son of Charles Edward Haviland, was an artist and operated his own decorating studio from about 1910 to 1924. He used various marks which included his full name. They are sometimes seen as a decoration mark on Haviland porcelain. It is noted that his marks were renewed by Bruchard in 1924 (Lesur and Tardy, 1967, p. 123) and continued until 1928 (d'Albis and Romanet, p. 141). See Plate 44 for an example of his work.

If there is an overglaze mark, but it does not say "Haviland," then the piece was decorated by a decorating firm (in France or the United States) which applied its own mark. Usually such pieces exhibit professional decoration and are of collector interest because of the particular studio or artist indicated on the piece. The American Pickard firm is a notable example from that era. Pickard pieces are quite collectable and usually expensive, but price is based on the unique "Pickard" decoration and not because the piece was made by a specific manufacturer (Haviland or others).

In the descriptions of photographs, all pieces are factory decorated unless noted otherwise. Because the same decorating mark was used by Haviland & Co. from 1876 to 1930 (see Mark 13), it is not necessary to repeat the presence of that mark in the description of each color photograph unless it is different.

Similarly, the same whiteware mark was used by the Theodore Haviland Company from 1894 to 1957 (see Mark 27), but different decorating marks were used over time. Therefore, only the decorating mark is described in the captions for those pieces except if the whiteware mark is different from the usual one.

I present no new titles for any patterns or blanks in the description of the photographs. Pattern or blank names are mentioned only if they were used originally by the Haviland companies (and taken from advertisements or catalogs), or if it is one of the several common popular names. It should be noted that at various times, the companies identified the same shape or blank with a different name. For example, the forms, "Cannele" and "Torse" both refer to the same shape. This is noted in the descriptions of examples of those pieces. I use the words, "form" and "shape" interchangeably instead of using "blank" to indicate the body design of the pieces.

A quotation from a Haviland advertisement (1878) perhaps best describes Haviland porcelain and emphasizes the unique ageless quality of porcelain. It is this inherent quality that enables us to collect and treasure today the Haviland of yesterday.

Haviland & Co make but one quality of porcelain. The body is pure Saint-Yrieix kaolin of the finest quality. The glaze is pure feldspathic rock.

Both body and glaze are fired at one time,--are *melted together*,--at a temperature of 1800 degrees centigrade or 3200 degrees Farenheit, a temperature at which all metals, except platina, are volatilized.

This porcelain therefore is the hardest and most dense material produced by human industry, and consequently the cleanest for usage and the most durable. Although porcelain of the best manufacture is expensive 100 francs worth will last much longer than the same value in cheapest pottery.

I hope you enjoy seeing the selection of collectable Haviland presented in the color photographs of this book following the next section on Haviland Marks. From these examples, it should be obvious that Haviland china deserves appreciation and collectability on merits more than merely pattern matching. Age, quality of craftsmanship, uniqueness of design and type of item plus beautiful decoration combine to make Haviland a prime example of late nineteenth and early twentieth century European china.

In addition to the color photographs, some black and white photographs of pieces from two old Haviland catalogs are shown on the following pages. The first group of pictures illustrates examples of the Haviland Art Pottery line made in Paris at the Auteuil studio from 1873 until 1882. The second set of photographs are of Sandoz and Poberejsky items made by the Theodore Haviland Company during the 1920's. Articles illustrated in old catalogs are extremely useful for they identify objects that were definitely manufactured. Thus, collectors can be aware of certain pieces needed to complete a collection. I thank Audrey and Dan Shanahan for providing these photographs and sharing this information with Haviland collectors.

Tarif Des Faiences

(Catalog Illustrations of Haviland Art Pottery)

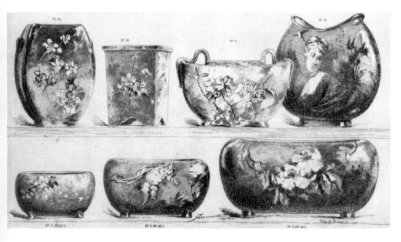

Catalog Illustrations of Theodore Haviland's
Sandoz and Poberejsky Porcelain

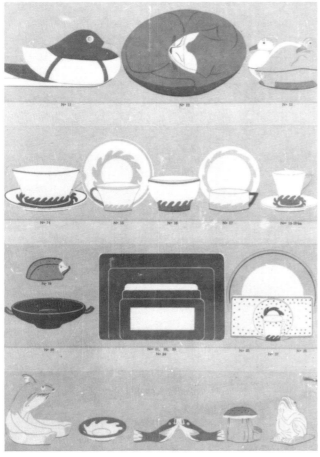

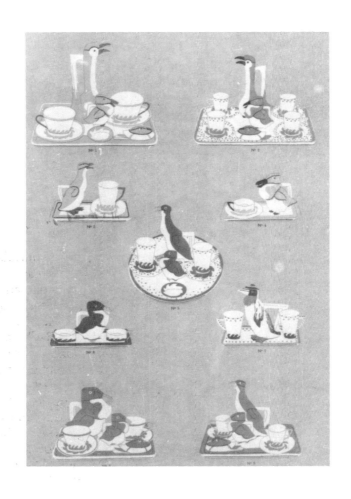

Haviland Marks

The marks found on Haviland products chronicle the history of the company as well as the various titles under which the firm has operated. But the marks, although reflecting the titles, are not identical to the firm name in all instances.

The section on marks in the several references listed in the bibliography have conflicting and contrasting information regarding the time period for some of the Haviland marks. After comparing information on Haviland marks from various works, I have based my dates for Haviland marks presented here primarily on two sources: a sheet of printed marks (published in Paris by Impressions Andre Rousseau, S. A., without a date) furnished by Audrey Shanahan who obtained the copy from the Haviland Company in Limoges; and marks shown for the companies by d'Albis and Romanet (pp. 239, 240, 243). I present some marks which are not shown by either of those sources; but based on my research, these marks can be dated within a certain period.

The major mistake apt to be made in dating marks found on any type of pottery is to infer that the listed date for a mark is a precise date. If only one date is shown for a mark, it appears that the mark was used only during one year. In most instances, the date simply indicates the first time the mark was used and then continued.

It is important to realize that the majority of marks on pottery cannot be dated to a precise year. Sometimes we are able to know when a mark was last used and another subsequent mark initiated. There is usually some overlapping, however. In many instances, we are presented with information concerning only the beginning and closing dates of a firm. That may be quite helpful, if the time span is short, but practically useless if the time span is for several years.

Although dating Haviland marks does not present as many problems as some other companies, the information is not without some confusion. Some information has been misinterpreted in some instances also. In one reference, I found a Haviland mark dated as "after 1797," an obvious error. I do not know if that was in fact a printer's error or whether it was intentional. Sometimes manufacturers or writers researching company histories show a date which reflects the time an earlier company had been in business at the same location or factory. Companies change

hands, or new owners take over premises where porcelain has been made at earlier times. But the date of the founding of the first company should not be used as a guide for dating a later company's products. Such a method of dating is really not only confusing, but is misleading.

According to d'Albis and Romanet (p. 237), the Limoges porcelain factories which were established after the French Revolution did not mark their products until around 1850. The practice of marking was not used widely until the last quarter of the nineteenth century. Therefore no marks are noted for the Haviland Company until the early 1850s, even though David Haviland had been decorating porcelain in Limoges since 1847.

I have divided Haviland marks into five categories to organize both the discussion of the marks and their photographs presented later in the book: (I) Haviland Brothers from the early 1850s until 1865; (II) Haviland & Co., from 1865-1876; (III) Haviland & Co., from 1876-1930; (IV) Theodore Haviland Company from 1892-1945; and (V) Post World War II marks.

I. Haviland Bros. & Co. early 1850s until 1865: Marks 1-4

Although David Haviland was not associated with Haviland Bros. after 1863, it is reasonable to assume that the same marks were continued for a short time, until about 1865, when his own factory began producing porcelain. Therefore the marks used from circa the early 1850s to 1865 consisted of the "Haviland" name either impressed on a separate piece of porcelain and attached to the base of items (see Marks 1-3), or impressed directly into the base of the items (see Mark 4). Items marked in this fashion were made especially for the Haviland Bros. Co. by other Limoges factories. Presumably, then, the porcelain was decorated by the Haviland decorating studio in Limoges.

Sometimes one sees a piece of porcelain with one of these marks whose decoration appears to be later than 1865. The reason for this is because all pieces were not decorated immediately after being made. But if there is the impressed name of "Haviland" on the piece, it was *made* before 1865, even though it may have been decorated later (see Plate 18 for an example). The type and method of decoration may help to indicate when the piece was actually decorated if there is no additional overglaze mark on the piece. The impressed full name marks would not have been continued after 1865, because Haviland Bros. was no longer in business, and it would have only been natural for David Haviland to design new marks to reflect the changing title of his business in Limoges.

II. Haviland & Cie., about 1865-1876: Mark 5

After David Haviland's factory began production, pieces were sometimes marked with an impressed mark of "H & Co" (see Mark 5). This mark reflects the change of the firm's title and also the first period of porcelain both manufactured and decorated by the Haviland firm. It is interesting that d'Albis and Romanet (p. 239) note that only "some" pieces were marked. The reason all pieces were not marked can be found in *White House China* by Margaret Klapthor (1975, p. 177). A footnote contains a letter written on 4 March 1869 by Charles Edward Haviland to his brother Theodore in New York:

"It would certainly be a good thing to stamp all our china with our name if: 1st our china was better than any one else or at least as good and 2nd if we made enough for our trade. Without that it would turn against us and learn people that by ordering through Vogt or Nittal they could get Gibus and Julieus china which is better than ours. And if ours was the best but we did not make enough to fill orders there would be a complaint when we gave other manufacturer's china. So our first aim must be to manufacture as well or better than anybody else and to make all we sell. *Then & then only* it will be a capital thing to stamp all our make with our name."

Please note that in the passage just quoted, "Julieus" is not the correct spelling of the Limoges potter named Jullien. Because Klapthor was quoting from a handwritten letter, the last part of the name was not easily deciphered. Indeed, d'Albis and Romanet (p. 92) also quote a different letter written in 1865 by Charles Haviland in which the potter's name was spelled "Julien." Thus Klapthor's apparent error of "ieus" for "ien" would have been easy to commit.

Klapthor (p. 24) shows a picture of a mark which she believes to be the first printed Haviland mark. "Haviland & Cie." over "Limoges" in an oval shape is printed in a red-orange color. She notes that this mark was found on one dessert saucer in a service made for President Grant about 1870 plus on a privately owned set of porcelain. Evidently this was a rare mark. It is not shown by the other sources I have checked.

III. Haviland & Co., 1876-1930: Marks 6-22

A little more than ten years elapsed before the Haviland Company felt secure enough in the quality of its porcelain

to mark all of its products. The system of marking adopted by Haviland & Co. in 1876 was to use two forms of printed marks: one underglaze in green, using initials to denote company of manufacture, and one overglaze, in various colors, containing the full name of the company to denote factory decoration.

Sometimes examples are seen with both the impressed mark of "H & Co" with a printed mark of H & Co (see

L
Mark 9). If one looks carefully, it will be seen that the printed mark is overglaze rather than underglaze, meaning that it was applied after the piece had been made. In most instances this double marking is found on toilet items or more utilitarian pieces. It is probable that pieces marked in this fashion were made after 1875, although as mentioned earlier, it was not uncommon for whiteware to be made at one time, placed in inventory, and then decorated later. But from examples of various pieces so marked, apparently the impressed mark of "H & Co" overlapped with the printed marks which were begun in 1876.

Underglaze Marks. The first underglaze printed marks were "H & Co" either alone or underscored with one or two lines (1876-1880, see Marks 6-8). Also from 1876 to 1889, H & Co was used (see Mark 9). A mark of H & Co

L   Depose
is noted to have been instituted in 1887, however no information is available on how long that mark was used (see Mark 10, "Depose" means patented). A similar mark to that shown in Mark 9 was adopted in 1888 (see Mark 11). There is no underscoring of "H & Co" and the word "FRANCE" was added to the mark. This mark was in use from 1888 to 1896. In about 1893, a mark of "Haviland" written in a semi-curved shape over "France" was begun (see Mark 12). That mark was the underglaze mark used for the longest period of time--from 1893 to 1930--when the company closed. Note the overlapping of time periods for these different marks.

Overglaze Marks. The principal overglaze mark used by Haviland & Co was "Haviland & Co" written in a crescent shape over "Limoges" in red from 1876 to 1930. (Sometimes one sees the mark in colors other than red-- see Marks 13 and 14.) During this period, however, several other overglaze marks were used at various times for short periods. One was a black mark of "H & Co, Depose" superimposed over a bird with spread wings (see d'Albis and Romanet, p. 239). That is considered a very rare mark, used seemingly only in 1878 as that is the only date indicated by the references. An overglaze mark, "Haviland & Co" was also used for a short time--1876 to 1878. This mark was in black, blue, green, or reddish-brown (see Mark 16). A manufacturers information sheet also notes that a decorating mark of H & Co (like the underglaze mark in

L
Mark 9) was used in the same colors during the same time. A double circle mark containing the name "Haviland & Co,

Limoges'' was used from 1879 to 1889 in several colors (see Marks 17 and 18).

Two other marks (''Special'' and ''Elite'') are very scarce. They were used only from 1878 to 1883 and they were made on paper labels. Some references show these marks but do not indicate that they were paper labels. It is no wonder that such are rarely seen. These stickers were actually used to grade the quality of the porcelain. A Haviland advertisement (1879) for ordering merchandise explains the use of these paper marks. It states that of 100 finished pieces, an average of 25 were taken out because they were inferior in quality. The other 75 percent were graded as follows: Special, 5%, was reserved for ''very best decoration,'' and contained the paper label of H & Co written in
Special
reddish-brown; the second best category (''Elite''; 15%) had a similar paper label of H & Co written in green (see Mark 19). These pieces were recommended for ''best selection.'' The third category (''Choix''; 25%) was marked with just the underglaze green whiteware mark of H & Co. These
L
pieces were noted as suitable for ordinary use. The fourth category (''2nd Choix''; 30%) was either unmarked or marked with a diagonal cross-bar through the green underglaze whiteware mark. This fourth category was recommended to be the most economical pottery and ''. . . is less imperfect than the best porcelain sent from China and Japan.''

Customers ordering porcelain could designate which class of porcelain they wanted, and their choice of decoration would then be applied to that particular quality with the price for the same decoration increasing or decreasing according to the class chosen. ''Choix'' was the class with the base price; ''2nd Choix'' was 15% less than the base; ''Elite'' was 20% more than the base; and ''Special'' was 50% more than the base. The information further states that ''on '2nd Choix' the decoration will be made by our least paid artists, while on 'Elite' the decorations will be made by our best painters and decorators. Decorations on 'Special' selection are entrusted to exceptional artists.''

Today, it is of course impossible to know in which of these classes an example made during that period might have been graded, unless, by chance, one of the paper labels remained intact. This method of ordering of course was intended for wholesalers or retail outlets and not for individual customers.

Other Haviland & Co. Marks. The art pottery and stoneware made in Paris from 1873 to 1886 were also marked. These marks were impressed: ''H & Co'' or ''Haviland & Co'' over ''Limoges'' (see Marks 20-22). The paper label of the exclusive outlet for the art pottery, L'Escalier de Cristal (glass staircase) is shown in Mark 21 also.

IV. Theodore Haviland Company, 1892-1945: Marks 23-35

Although the Theodore Haviland Company was established in 1892, one of the marks appears to either predate the establishment of the firm, or the firm's production of porcelain. This mark consists of the initials ''T'' over ''H'' enclosed in one solid line circle and another outer circle composed of pointed triangular shapes. The mark is in red overglaze and is clearly a decorating mark (see Mark 23). This mark could reflect a decorating mark used by Theodore while he was still associated with his brother Charles at Haviland & Co., or it could be a mark used before his own company was in full production. No whiteware mark appears on the piece I show (see Plate 123) to indicate the company that manufacatured the piece. However, the year 1894 is noted by d'Albis and Romanet (p. 239) as the first year a decorating mark was used by the company.

Underglaze Marks. The first factory underglaze mark for the Theodore Haviland Company is agreed to be the ''Mont-Mery'' mark (see Mark 24). That mark was adopted in 1892, according to all references. Most indicate that the mark was used only in 1892, and others just state the date without elaboration on whether it was used for only one year or longer. D'Albis and Romanet (p. 239) also show this mark with an 1892 date. However, they also state (on p. 141) that production of the new company did not begin until 1893. It is noted that Theodore's first endeavor after leaving Haviland & Co. was to set up a temporary studio for designing his first collection of models. Perhaps, it was this first collection that had the ''Mont-Mery'' mark. At any rate, another green underglaze mark is noted to have been used starting the next year, 1893 (see Mark 26). This mark is ''Th́eo. Haviland, Limoges, France.'' Note that Theodore is abbreviated. No information is available indicating whether this mark was used for only one year (1893) or continued after that year. From the few examples seen with either mark 24 or 26, it is reasonable to infer that these marks were used only for a short time. Another mark (see Mark 25) is similar to Mark 24 with the initials ''T.H.'' preceding ''HAVILAND'' over the same 3 castle towers, however, ''Mont-Mery'' is not included in this mark. I have placed it in this early category of Theodore Haviland marks because of its similarity to both marks 24 and 26.

The primary mark used by the Theodore Haviland Company to denote factory of manufacture was inaugurated in 1894 and used until 1957 (see Mark 27). This is an impressed rather than a printed mark. The initials ''T. H.'' separated by a legion of honor symbol constitute this mark.

Several underglaze printed marks designed by writing ''Theodore Haviland, France'' vertically in letters resembling Chinese characters were used during the early 1900s. Such marks are quite rare. They reflected Theodore's interest in Oriental art. No examples were available for photographing.

During the same time period (1894-1957) when the impressed initials were used to indicate factory manufacture, two other underglaze printed marks were used also. One was a horseshoe shaped mark of ''Theodore Haviland, France,'' from 1920 to 1936 (see Mark 29). Another was a shield mark containing his name with ''Limoges'' above, from 1936 to 1945 (see Mark 30). This latter mark is not frequently seen probably because its use was during the war years.

Overglaze Marks. The first decorating mark for the Theodore Haviland Company, initiated in 1894, was similar to the impressed mark of the "T. H." initials with the legion of Honor symbol (see Mark 31). "Porcelaine Mousseline" appeared over the initials. According to d'Albis and Romanet (p. 141), "Mousseline" was Theodore's term for describing the special paste or mixture his company made. Translated, the word means "silk." I show one version of this mark; others show the mark with the initials written horizontally, separated by the Legion of Honor symbol with "Limoges" written in script form under the "T" and "FRANCE" printed under the "H." This version of the mark is very similar to one adopted in 1895 (see Mark 32). The difference is that "Porcelaine" is printed below the Legion of Honor symbol, and the name is spelled out (Theodore Haviland) in lieu of initials, or "Theodore" is abbreviated to "Theo." Marks 31 and 32 appeared to have been used until about 1903.

In 1903 to circa 1925, an overglaze mark with "Theodore Haviland" written in printed script and slanted, with "Limoges" in written script and "FRANCE" printed was begun (see Mark 33). The same mark with the first name underscored is seen frequently (see Mark 34). Inexplicably only one French source (Lesur and Tardy, 1967, p. 127) shows this mark and dates it from 1926. American sources treat this mark variously: Wood (1951, p. 111) and Young (1970, p. 23) date it as 1914. Jacobson (1979, p. 17) dates it 1903. This mark, however, is shown in a 1904 catalog, and the same mark in an impressed rather than printed form (see Mark 28) is known (from examples with the mark) to have been used in 1904. Therefore, the underscored mark would date as early as 1904. It is evident from examples, especially noted by the mark on Sandoz items (which were manufactured from around 1915 to the mid 1920s) that the mark was used as late as the mid 1920s. I date it from about 1904 to about 1925.

A third mark looks similar to Marks 33 and 34 (see Mark 35), except there is no underscoring of the first name, and the full name is printed script, but straight aligned rather than slanted. This mark is dated by most as a 1920's mark; d'Albis and Romanet (p. 239) indicate 1925 as the first year of that mark. No information is available on when this mark was discontinued, but it was probably used until the early or mid 1940s.

V. Post-World War II: Marks 36-38

In 1948, a decorating mark of "Haviland's" with a pattern name under it was begun (see Mark 36). In 1958, another overglaze mark of a tower with "HAVILAND, LIMOGES, FRANCE" was adopted (see Mark 37). In 1967, a similar mark was established except only the first letter in "Haviland" was capitalized and the tower was revised.

As late as 1980, however, the mark originating in 1958 was apparently still being used (d'Albis and Romet, p. 243).

The old "Haviland" over "France" mark (see mark 12) with the addition of "Limoges" is also noted by d'Albis and Romanet to be a current whiteware mark. Recall that in 1941, William Haviland, Theodore's son, was able to regain the marks of Haviland & Co. which had been sold by his cousin, George, in 1931. With access to these older marks, William Haviland was able to revert to using the mark for products of the Theodore Haviland Company in France. According to d'Albis and Romanet (p. 240) the mark was used again from 1941 to 1962 (see Mark 37). It is not clear just when after 1941 the mark was put back in use. Evidently "Limoges" was added to the mark after 1962 which clearly makes it a different mark than the earlier one.

Seemingly, the reinstitution of the whiteware mark used from 1893 to 1930 could cause confusion when used on products after 1941. However, the overglaze decorating mark should eliminate this problem (see Mark 37 for an example). Also some contemporary Haviland does not have an underglaze whiteware mark, but only the overglaze decorating mark (see Mark 38).

Additional Explanations

To conclude the discussion on Haviland marks, a few other points should be emphasized. One is that most sources note that the word "France" was added to the Haviland marks in 1891 to comply with the American tarrif laws. However, as was true with other European and Limoges pottery manufacturers, some firms showed the country of origin in marks prior to that time. According to d'Albis and Romanet (p. 239), "France" was added to Haviland marks in 1888 (see Mark 11).

There has been some question over whether the Haviland Company ever used a mark of just "H & C" (without the letter "o" for company). One French reference (Lesur and Tardy, 1967, p. 125) attributes two such marks to the Haviland Company. In discussions with Jean d'Albis, Audrey Shanahan informs me that such a mark is not considered by the Haviland historian ever to have been used by the Haviland Company. Evidence to support D'Albis' opinion is that other Limoges companies either used the English abbreviation "Co." for company or the French "Cie." I have not found any Limoges firm which used the letter "C" to designate "company," although other European porcelain manufacturers did. Of course, the letter "o" (whether printed or incised) is small in such marks and not easy to see.

Sometimes an English diamond shaped registry mark is seen in conjunction with Haviland marks. Some people argue that such a mark was used by David Haviland in order that Americans would purchase the French-made tableware, thinking it was English. They suggest that Americans were biased and would only accept English products. Neither is correct. That particular method of marking English ceramics was begun in England in 1843 and continued until 1884. The registration was to protect a mold or decoration pattern for a period of three years. Companies in other countries exporting to England could register their patterns and designs with the English office and mark their wares with the special mark. Therefore, Haviland registered some of his molds or patterns and marked them with the English registry mark. Remember that Haviland exported to England and other countries as well as America. Books on English marks show tables which can be used to decipher these marks, but please be aware that the date of registration only means the date that the design was *first* registered, and the same mark might be used for some years after that time. Often such marks, however, are difficult or impossible to read, especially if they are impressed (see Mark 15).

In many instances additional overglaze marks are seen with those of the Haviland decorating marks. Usually the second overglaze mark indicates various American (or some other country) importers, distributors, department stores, or even certain individuals. Having the Haviland companies add the purchaser's firm name to the products lent a note of prestige for the businesses (or individuals). See Mark 15 for an example of a well-known American importer during the late 1800s.

In the photographs of Marks, please note that Marks 6 through 12 are intended to show and describe only the *underglaze* mark in initial form, so please ignore the overglaze mark; likewise, in Marks 13 through 18, the marks are intended to show and describe only the *overglaze* decorating (or other) mark, so please ignore the underglaze marks. The close proximity of the overglaze mark to the underglaze mark made it impossible in most cases to photograph only one of the marks.

Haviland Marks Early 1850s to 1930

Mark 1. Applied mark of impressed name, indicates pieces made for Haviland Bros. by other Limoges companies, but presumably decorated by the Haviland studio, early 1850s to about 1865.

Mark 2. Applied mark of impressed name, similar to Mark 1, early 1850s to about 1865.

Mark 3. Applied mark of impressed name with "Depose," similar to Marks 1 and 2, mid 1850s to about 1865.

Mark 4. Impressed name, not attached but impressed directly into base, mid 1850s to about 1865.

Mark 5. Impressed initials, used during first period of porcelain manufacture by Haviland & Cie., 1865-1875.

Mark 6. Underglaze initials in green, 1876-1880.

Mark 7. Underglaze initials in green, underscored, 1876-1880.

Mark 8. Underglaze initials in green, underscored with two lines, 1876-1880.

Mark 9. Underglaze initials in green, underscored with "L" added to indicate "Limoges," 1876-1889. Note: this same mark was used overglaze as a decorating mark in various colors for a short time from about 1878.

Mark 10. Underglaze, initials in green, underscored with "Depose," adopted about 1887.

Mark 11. Underglaze, initials in green with "L" for "Limoges" and "FRANCE," 1888-1896.

Mark 12. Underglaze, full name with "France," in green, 1893-1930.

Mark 13. Overglaze full name with "Limoges" in red, 1876-1930. Note: presence of an overglaze mark indicates factory decoration.

Mark 14. Same as Mark 13, in blue, 1876-1930. "Feu de Four" added to indicate special firing technique. Red overglaze mark indicates pieces were made for the "R. B. Gray Co., St. Louis," Missouri.

Mark 15. Overglaze in red, importer mark of "Davis, Collamore, & Co. Importers, 24.7 Broadway, New York." Also impressed English Registry Mark, indicating particular design had been registered with the English Registry Office.

Mark 16. Overglaze in blue, full name, 1876-1878.

Mark 17. Overglaze, in blue (or other colors) double circle mark with full name, 1879-1889.

Mark 18. Overglaze in green, same as Mark 17, 1879-1889.

Mark 19. Round paper label with initials over "Elite" in green, 1878-1883. This mark was used to grade the whiteware, but it is overglaze. Another similar mark of "Special" under "H & Co" in reddish-brown was used at the same time. It is extremely rare to find examples with these paper marks.

Mark 20. Impressed full name underscored with "Limoges," art pottery mark, 1873-1882.

Mark 21. Impressed initials, art pottery mark, 1873-1882. Also paper label for L'Escalier de Cristal, exclusive outlet for the Haviland art pottery.

Mark 22. Impressed initials on stoneware with Chaplet's artist mark symbolizing a rosary, 1882-1886.

Theodore Haviland Marks 1892 to 1945

Mark 23. Overglaze decorating mark, initials, in red, before 1892.

Mark 24. Underglaze, in green, "Mont-Mery" over three castle towers, initials, "FRANCE," c. 1892.

Mark 25. Underglaze, in green, "TH. HAVILAND" over three castle towers, "Limoges" in script, "FRANCE" printed, c. early 1890s (probably after 1892).

Mark 26. Underglaze, in green, "Théo. Haviland," with "Limoges" in script, "FRANCE" printed, c. 1893.

Mark 27. Impressed initials with the Legion of Honor symbol, primary whiteware mark used to identify factory from 1894 to 1957.

Mark 28. Impressed full name with "Théodore" underscored, the same design as overglaze Mark 34, c. 1904 to mid 1920s.

Mark 29. Underglaze, full name written in horseshoe shape, with "FRANCE" in center of mark, in green, c. 1920-1936.

Mark 30. Underglaze, full name with "FRANCE" in shield shape with "Limoges" in rectangular shape above, c. 1936-1945.

Mark 31. Overglaze, in green, initials with "Porcelaine Mousseline" separated by Legion of Honor symbol and "FRANCE," in circular shape, 1894-1903. Mark also was written horizontally with "Limoges" in script form under the initial "T." and "FRANCE" printed under the initial "H." 1894-1903.

Mark 32. Overglaze, in red, full name with the Legion of Honor symbol (may appear with "Theodore" abbreviated to "Théo."), 1895 to probably 1903.

Mark 33. Overglaze, in red, full name in printed script, slanted, with "Limoges" in written script, and FRANCE printed, 1903-1925.

Mark 34. Overglaze, in red, same as in Mark 33, except "Theodore" is underscored, c. 1904 to mid 1920s.

Mark 35. Overglaze, in red, similar to Marks 33 and 34, except the name is written with the letters straight aligned rather than slanted, 1925 to probably mid 1940s.

Post World War II Marks, Haviland S. A.

Mark 36. Overglaze, "Haviland's" with pattern name printed underneath, c. 1948.

Mark 37. Underglaze, in green, same as Mark 12, but reinstituted in 1941 and used to c. 1962; overglaze mark of a tower with "HAVILAND, LIMOGES, FRANCE" with a pattern name. The overglaze mark was adopted c. 1958 and is also a contemporary mark.

Mark 38. Overglaze, in red, similar to Mark 37 but without "FRANCE," after 1967. Note that some contemporary porcelain, as this example, does not have an underglaze mark, but only the overglaze mark.

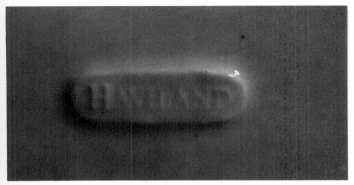

Mark 1

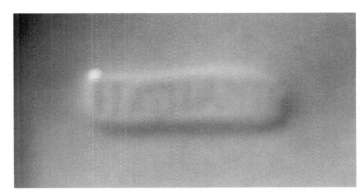

Mark 2

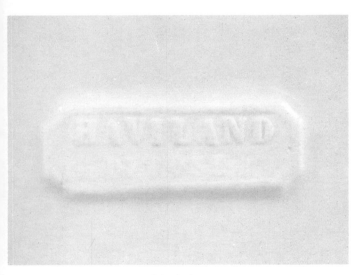

Mark 3

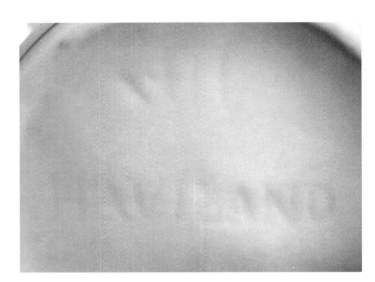

Mark 4

Mark 5

Mark 6

Mark 7

Mark 8

Mark 9

Mark 10

Mark 11

Mark 12

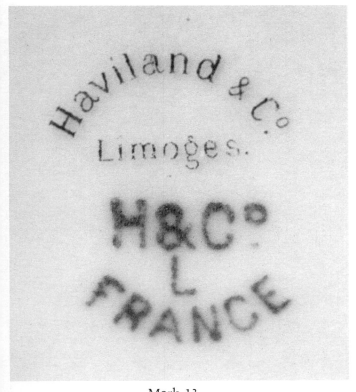

Mark 13

Mark 14

Mark 15

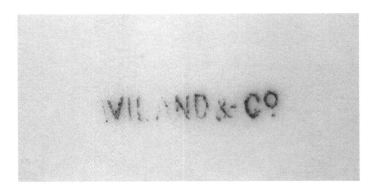

Mark 16

Mark 17

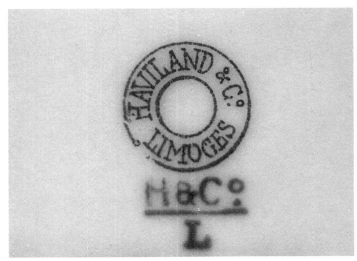

Mark 18

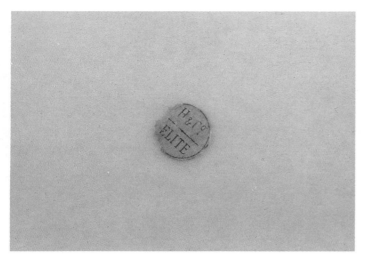

Mark 19

Mark 20

Mark 21

Mark 22

Mark 23

Mark 24

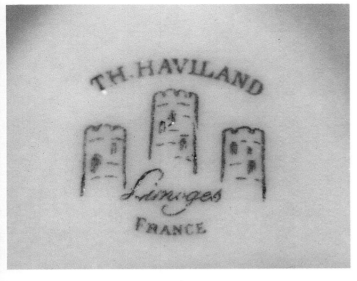

Mark 25

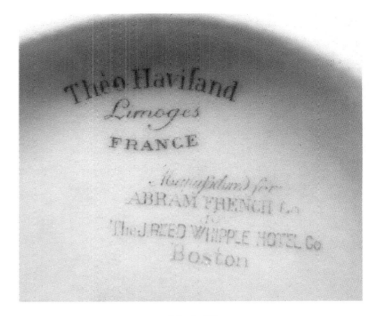

Mark 26

Mark 27

Mark 28

Mark 29

Mark 30

Mark 31

Mark 32

Mark 33

Mark 34

Mark 35

Mark 36

Mark 38

Mark 37

Plate 1. Coffee Pot, Mark 2, 10½″h, unique Haviland design, undecorated, rare.

Plate 2. Vase, Mark 3, 16½″h, scenic design by artist, Saquet, gold applied by Dominique with embossed floral decor on cobalt blue background, one of a pair. One of several designs shown at the Crystal Palace at New York World's Fair in 1853 which won the gold medal for Haviland, rare. (Shanahan Collection)

Plate 3. Matching Vase to Plate 2.

Plate 4. Elephant Humidor, Mark 1, 8″h, original designs created by the ceramicist Samson and displayed in Paris and Limoges in 1855. All designs were of oriental or East Indian subjects. Examples of these humidors are very rare, with only 3, each different, known to exist. (Shanahan Collection)

Plate 5. Vase, Mark 3, 14¾"h, cobalt blue porcelain with gold leaf and floral decor with applied white bisque floral vine in high relief, rare. (Shanahan Collection)

Plate 6. Teapot, Mark 3, 7½"h, simple gold band decoration.

Plate 7. Water Pitcher, Mark 1, 10"h, embossed floral designs, handpainted, gold trim.

Plate 8. Coffee Pot, Mark 3, 9"h, curved split handle, wide gold band decor.

Plate 9. Coffee Pot, Mark 3, 8"h, scalloped spout, gold trim.

Plate 10. Gravy Boat with separate Underplate, Mark 3, 6¼″h, from dinner service called "Red-Edge" in "Ivy" form; note teardrop shape of underplate. The use of the color red in decorating was not common during this period of the mid 1850s (see Plates 11 and 12 for examples of other pieces in the set). (Shanahan Collection)

Plate 11. Covered Sauce Tureen in "Red-Edge" decor, acorn finial, additional gold trim.

Plate 12. Pot-de-Creme Service for four from "Red-Edge" set, 3¾″h, ea., two-tiered pedestal stand. These are for baking and serving dessert custard.

Plate 13. Tea or Dessert Set, Mark 3, "Ivy" form, green and gold decoration. Cake Plate, 11"d; Cup, 2½"h; Saucer, 5¾"d; Teapot with acorn finial, 9"h.

Plate 14. Sugar and Teapot, Mark 3, embossed designs, gold trim.

Plate 15. Creamer, 7"h, and Sugar, 8"h, Mark 3, gold band decor.

Plate 16. Footbath, Mark 3, 21″l, 11″ deep. 13″w, 25 lbs. empty. Wide gold band at top and base and inside and handles enhanced with gold trim (note ornate handle), rare. (Shanahan Collection)

Plate 17. Another view of Footbath in Plate 16.

47

Plate 18. Pitcher, Mark 4, "Moss Rose" design (popular name), gold trim. Note from the type of transfer decoration on this piece, that it was decorated after 1865, although from the mark on the piece, it is evident that the pitcher was *made* before 1865.

Plate 19. Creamer, 5″h, Mark 4, scalloped top, gold trim.

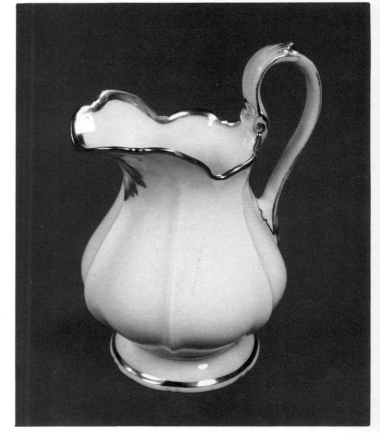

Plate 21. Covered Vegetable, Mark 5, 7"h, 11"d.

Plate 20. Mouth Rinse Ewer, Mark 5, 8"h, rose and daisies with hand enamelling over design.

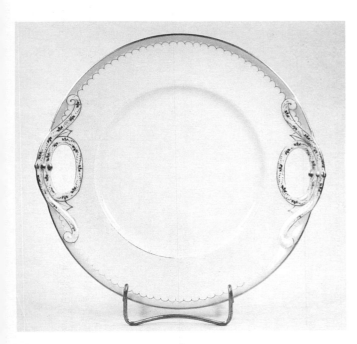

Plate 22. Cake Plate, Mark 5, 10"d.

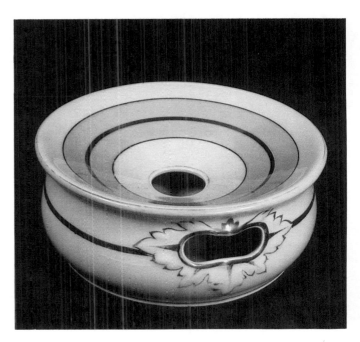

Plate 23. Cuspidor, Mark 5, 8½"d.

Plate 24. Wash Set, Mark 5 underglaze and Mark 9 overglaze, Bowl, 5″h, 15½″d; Pitcher, 12¼″h, wide red band decor outlined in gold (see Plate 25).

Plate 25. Matching accessories for Wash Set: Pitcher, 8″h; Soap Dish, 4″l, 4½″w with liner; Shaving Mug, 3″h; Flat Toothbrush Holder, 8″l. A complete set is quite rare. (Shanahan Collection)

50

Haviland Art Pottery, 1873-1886

Plate 26. Terra Cotta Gourd Vase, Mark 21, 7¼"h, floral decor, signed on lower right side, "HA". (Shanahan Collection)

Plate 27. Back of vase in Plate 26.

Plate 28. Terra Cotta Jug Vase, 14″h, by Edouard Lindeneher, signed in crust on side and in black on base, sculpted floral designs. (Shanahan Collection)

52

Plate 29. Terra Cotta Jardiniere, Mark 20 (with Haviland underscored), sculpted flowers, unsigned by artist, but attributed to Gérard. (Shanahan Collection)

Plate 30. Pair of Terra Cotta Vases, 12″h, sculpted flowers. (Shanahan Collection)

Plate 31. Terra Cotta Vase, 5″h, Marked H & Co over L, three footed, artist signed "Ǝ" artist unidentified. (Shanahan Collection)

Plate 32. Back of vase in Plate 31, note artist's signature.

Plate 33. Terra Cotta Vase, 5″h, Mark 21, artist signed "R." (Shanahan Collection)

54

Plate 34. Stoneware Jug, Mark 22, 5″h, artist signed by Chaplet, rosary mark indicates his signature in Mark 22. (Shanahan Collection)

Plate 35. Terra Cotta Vase, Mark 20, 12″h, 13″w, gold and silver on black lacquer foundation, dusted with gold, bird and florals, artist signed by Midoux. (Shanahan Collection)

Plate 36. Vase, 16½″h, by Edouard Lindeneher, signed on side and base in black, sculpted floral, leaf, and vine shapes. (Shanahan Collection)

Special Categories for Collectors

Plate 37. Napoleon Bonaparte and his Ladies, Mark 26, "Vincennes" form, Portrait Service, handpainted, artist signed, "L. Jean." Service consists of Charger, 12¾"d plus twelve individual 9" plates (see Plates 39-44), rare. (Shanahan Collection)

Plate 38. Josephine and Marie Louise.

Plate 39. Mlle de Sombreiul and Dse d'Angouleme.

Plate 40. Reine Hortense and Dse de Berry.

Plate 41. Mme de Stael and Mme Roland.

Plate 42. Mme de Récamier and Pauline Bonaparte (Napoleon's sister).

Plate 43. Mme de Genlin and Carolyn Bonaparte (Napoleon's sister).

Plate 44. Miniature Tea Set, Mark 12 with Frank Haviland's decorating mark, Tea Pot, 5"h, Sugar Basket, 3½"l, 2½"w; creamer, 2"h; tray 12"l, 8"w, rare.

Plate 45. Miniature Chocolate Pot, Mark 12 with Mark 13 in gold, 5"h.

Plate 46. Miniature Chocolate Pot, Mark 12, 5¼"h.

Plate 48. Salesman's sample, Mark 9 with decorating mark of factory artist, "M. G. H." Cup, 2¼"h, Saucer, 5¾"d, Orchids and Dragonflys.

Plate 47. Salesman's sample, Chocolate Pot, Mark 9, 9½"h, "Diana" form (numbers on base such as "T..46..," etc., indicate other shapes in which the piece could be ordered).

Plate 49. Aurene Glass, 3½"h, marked "Haviland & Co.," painted in white on the base. This art glass in various pieces was manufactured by French glassmakers and marked with the Haviland mark during the mid 1870s and 1880s. Examples are very collectable. (Shanahan Collection)

Plate 50. Oyster Plate, 9"d, "Presidential" form, patented August 10, 1880. This plate is a replica from the famous Haviland dinner service made for President Rutherford B. Hayes The designs for the service were made by the noted American illustrator, Theodore R. Davis. Marine, animal, and nature themes were used to decorate the items. Replicas of pieces are in high demand. Examples have a facsimile of Davis' signature and a seal of the United States (or the Arms of the Dominion for the Canadian market) on the back. Davis did not actually paint the pieces; the signature is to denote his designs. (Shanahan Collection)

Plate 51. Collector Plate in Kate Greenaway style, Mark 6, 9½"d, "Basketweave" or "Tresse" Mold. One from a service of 12, each with different captions on the back. Example shown is "Little Maid, Pretty Maid, Whither Goest Thou."

Plate 52. Railroad China, Mark 12, made for The New York Central Lines, Ice Cream Shell, "De Pew" pattern, 5¾"l, 5"w.

Plate 53. Railroad China, Mark 12, made for Kansas City Missouri for the Burlington Route, Platter, 9¼"l, 6¼"w, "Violets and Daisies" pattern was a trademark for the Chicago, Burlington, and Quincy lines. American potteries as well as Haviland made this particular pattern for the company.

Plate 54. Railroad China, Mark 34, made for Northern Pacific Railroad Co., Platter, 11½"l, 7¾"w, rare. (Shanahan Collection)

Plate 55. Railroad China, Mark 33, made for Chicago, Milwaukee, St. Paul Line, Cup, 2"h, Saucer 5¾"d.

Plate 56. Club Ware, Mark 11, United States Naval Insignia, One Handled Egg Cup, 3"h, Saucer, 6¼"d.

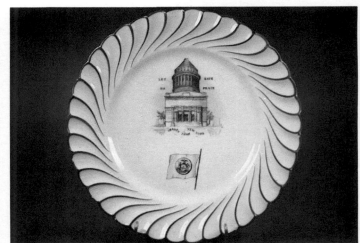

Plate 57. Commemorative Plate, Mark 11, made for and distributed by the R.H. Macy Co., New York, 9"d, "Cannelé" or "Torse" form, transfer design of Grant's Tomb with the inscription "Let Us Have Peace."

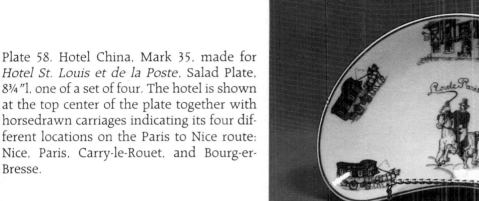

Plate 58. Hotel China, Mark 35, made for *Hotel St. Louis et de la Poste*, Salad Plate, 8¾"l, one of a set of four. The hotel is shown at the top center of the plate together with horsedrawn carriages indicating its four different locations on the Paris to Nice route: Nice, Paris, Carry-le-Rouet, and Bourg-er-Bresse.

Plate 59. Hotel China, Mark 10, made for the Grand Pacific Hotel, Chicago, Plate, 9½"d, "Club du Barry" shape, gold decor on cobalt blue.

Plate 60. Hotel China Spooner, Mark 26, 6"h, for the "J. Reed Whipple Hotel Co., New York."

Plate 61. Advertising China, Mark 29, Ash Tray, 4½"l, 3"w, for Pigall's, Paris-Montmartre.

Plate 62. Sandoz Item, Mark 34, Monkey Tobacco Jar, 7"h, artist signed. This particular piece is unique and rare because it is not a tableware item as most other Sandoz pieces. (Shanahan Collection)

Plate 64. Sandoz Item, Mark 34, Fishes Knife Rest, 5″l. (Shanahan Collection)

Plate 63. Sandoz Item, Duck Pitcher, Mark 34, artist signed. (Shanahan Collection)

Plate 65. Sandoz Items, Marks 29 and 34, Creamer, 4½″h, Individual Coffee Pot, 5½″h. (Shanahan Collection)

Plate 66. Sandoz Item, Mark 34, Pequin Tea Pot, 5¾″h, artist signed. (Shanahan Collection)

Plate 67. Cavalier Bust, Mark 35 (see Plate 68 for marks on back), bisque, artist signed, "Champigny," 11½"h, 10½"w, very rare. (Shanahan Collection)

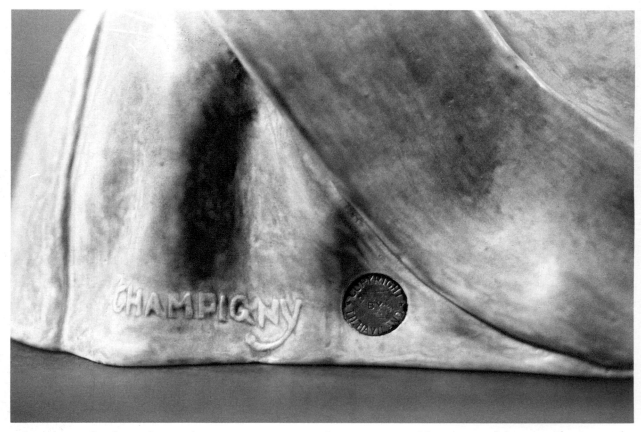

Plate 68. Back of Cavalier with artist's signature, "Champigny," and bronze medal stamped "Copyright by TH Haviland."

Plate 69. Basket, Mark 12, Handpainted violets not factory decorated.

Plate 70. Bon-Bon Basket, Mark 34, "Fantaisie Romeo" form.

Plate 71. Chamberstick, Mark 11, 3"h, 5½"d, tiny rosebuds and flowers with dark blue and gold edging. "Marseille" shape.

Plate 72. Basket, Mark 12, 5¼"l, 4"w, floral and clover designs.

Plate 74. Match Box, Mark 11, 1″h, 4″l, "Marseille" shape.

Plate 73. Liquor Decanter, underglaze mark like Mark 38, with "Haviland, Limoges" in red overglaze, 8½″h, "Chantilly" pattern.

Plate 75. Ferner, Mark 12, factory handpainted, artist signed, "Henri," 2½″h, 7½″d. This item also has a separate liner (not shown); examples with liners are scarce and thus more expensive than those without liners.

Plate 76. Candlestick, Mark 12, 7″h, "Ranson" shape.

Plate 77. Vase, Mark 12, 11″h, 3 handled with different floral designs on each side, hand enamelled. (Shanahan Collection)

Plate 78. Powder Box, 2″h, 4½″d, Mark 12, "Star" form, floral designs with gold and green trim, scarce item.

Plate 79. Hair Receiver, Mark 12, 5″l, 4″w, scarce.

Plate 80. Shaving Mug, Mark 6, 3¼″h.   •

Plate 81. Ring Tree, Mark 11, 4¼″l, 3″h, yellow florals with gold trim.

Plate 82. Vase, Mark 12, 12″h, handpainted, artist signed "O. Duringer," not factory decorated.

Plate 83. Back of Vase in Plate 82.

Plate 84. Vase, Mark 12, 12″h, handpainted rose decor on front and back, not factory decorated.

Plate 85. Back of Vase in Plate 84.

Plate 86. Vase, Mark 9, "Marseille" form, 8½"h, cream bisque finish.

Plate 87. Vase, Mark 12, 7"h, 3 handled, pink and blue marbled effect, handpainted, not factory decorated.

Plate 88. Vase, Mark 12, 12"h, 3 handled, large roses, gold handles, handpainted, not factory decorated.

Plate 89. Vase, Mark 9, 13¼"h, "Marseille" form, cobalt blue with gold, made for and noted on back "The George H. Forbes, New Haven." (Shanahan Collection)

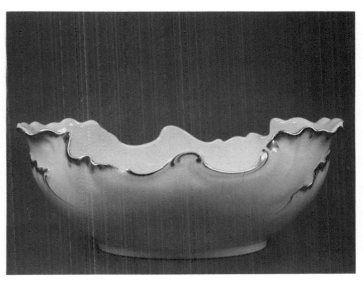

Plate 90. Jardiniere, Mark 9, 12″l, 8″w, footed, "Cannele" or "Torse" shape, hand enamelled over transfer floral designs.

Plate 91. Jardiniere, Mark 12, 9¾″l, 4″h, "Marseille" form. Note: this Jardiniere was made in 4 different sizes.

Plate 92. Center of Ormulu Mounted Compote (see Plate 93).

Plate 93. Ormolu Mounted Compote, Mark 12, 7″l, 5½″w, footed, figural center design with deep burgundy border and gold tracery.

Tableware and Accessories

Plate 94. Berry Set, Mark 9. Master Bowl, 9½"l, 7½"w; Individual Bowls, 5¼"d, "Diana" form, hand enamelled flower in each piece, silver handles on Master Bowl.

Plate 95. Bon-Bon Plate, Mark 12, 9"d, "Marseille" form, pierced at top.

Plate 96. Covered Bouillon, Mark 12, "Portia" form, burgundy and gold decor with enamelled center rose on saucer and in bottom of cup.

Plate 97. Covered Bouillon, Mark 12, Cup, 3½"h, Saucer, 5½"d, "Crystal" form.

Plate 98. Butter Pats: "Silver" form, Mark 12, 3¼"d; "Nenuphar" form, Mark 9, 3"sq; "Diana" form, Mark 11, 3"d.

Plate 99. Butter Tub, Mark 34, 1"h, 3½"d; Underplate, 6½"d.

Plate 100. Cake Plate, Mark 34, 12"l, 8½"d, "Satsuma" form, "Her Majesty" pattern, hand enamelled, signed "Fortin."

Plate 101. Cake Stand, Mark 11, 2"h, 9"d, "Marseille" form.

Plate 102. Chocolate Pot, Mark 11, 10"h, "Richelieu" form.

Plate 103. Chocolate Pot, Mark 12, 8"h, "Star" form.

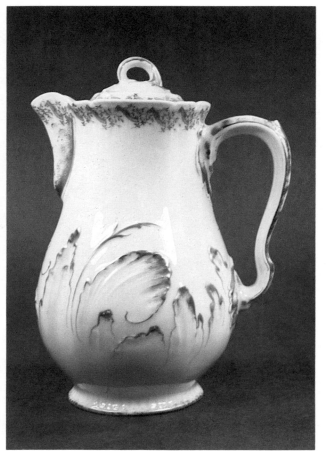

Plate 104. Chocolate Pot, Mark 26, 10"h.

Plate 105. Chocolate Pot, Mark 33, 11"h, "St. Germaine" form.

Plate 106. Chocolate Pot, Mark 12, 8″h, very popular "Baltimore Rose" pattern (popular name). (Shanahan Collection)

Plate 107. Chocolate Pot, Mark 11, 10″h, pink and green roses.

Plate 108. Chocolate Pot, Mark 9, 7¼″h, "Epi Haut" form.

Plate 109. Chocolate Pot, Mark 9, 8½″h, "Henry II" form, mixed floral designs with gold.

Plate 110. Chocolate Set, Mark 11, "Marseille" form: Tray, 14"sq.; creamer, 3½"h; sugar, 1½"h, 5½"d; Pot, 9"h; Cup, 3"h; Saucer 5"h, rare in complete set. (Shanahan Collection)

Plate 111. Chocolate Set, Mark 12, "Ranson" form, "Baltimore Rose" pattern (popular name): Tray, 18"l, 18"w; Pot, 10½"h, 6 cups and saucers. This pattern in gold is particularly rare in addition to a complete set being rare. (Shanahan Collection)

Plate 112. Chocolate Pot, Mark 9, 9″h, "Anchor" form, birds, butterflies, and flowers, hand enamelled.

Plate 113. Chocolate Pot, Mark 11, 9¼″h, with "Feu de Four" mark which means "fired longer" to give the pattern a special color, "Ranson" form, poppy decor. This particular pattern in "Feu de Four" is in much demand.

Plate 114. Chocolate Pot, Mark 12, 8″h, "Star" form, floral and gold decor.

Plate 115. Claret Jug, Mark 9, 5½″h, "Vermicella" form, made for Tiffany's of New York. Design of flowers, grasses and insects created by the artist Pallandre, hand enamelled.

Plate 116. Milk Pitcher, 7″h; Coffee Pot, 10½″h, Mark 12 on each, "Ranson" form, "The Norma" pattern.

Plate 117. Coffee Pot, Mark 34, 9"h, "Rouen" form.

Plate 118. Coffee Pot, Mark 11, 8½″h, "Pompadour" form.

Plate 119. Coffee Pot. Mark 33. 9¼"h. pink and white apple blossoms.

Plate 120. Coffee Pot, Mark 9, 10″h, rose finial.

Plate 121. Compote, Mark 11, 5¼″h, 9″d, "Marseille" form.

Plate 122. Compote, Mark 9, 7½″h, 9″d, "Lace" form, reticulated, two pieces fastened with bolt.

Plate 123. Compote, Mark 23, 8″h, 9″d, reticulated, floral design on base, rare Theodore Haviland decorating mark. (Shanahan Collection)

84

Plate 124. Compote, Mark 6 underglaze and Mark 17 overglaze, 5″h, 9″d, reticulated.

Plate 125. Cracker Jar, Mark 12, 7″h, "Ranson" form, hand-painted in Art Nouveau design, not factory decorated.

Plate 126. Cracker Jar, Mark 32, 7¼″h, "Rouen" form, violet decor.

Plate 127. Cracker Jar, Mark 11, 8″h, "Marseille" form, cobalt blue with gold.

Plate 128. Creamer, Mark 24, 6¼"h, rare "Mont-Mery" mark of Theodore Haviland. (Shanahan Collection)

Plate 129. Creamer & Sugar Set, Mark 9, "Cannele" form: Sugar, 3½"h, 8"w; Creamer, 4"h.

Plate 130. Dessert Creamer & Sugar, Mark 12, roses, enamelled: Sugar, 4½"l, 3"w; Creamer, 2½"h.

Plate 131. Demi-Tasse Cup, 2½"h; Saucer 5"d, Mark 13, bird and floral decor, gold beaded inner border.

Plate 132. Demi-Tasse Cup, 2½"h; Saucer, 5"d, Mark 9, "Club du Barry" form, green and yellow floral decor with center gold medallion.

Plate 133. Demi-Tasse Cup, 2"h; Saucer, 4¼"d, Mark 9, "Diana" form.

Plate 134. Demi-Tasse Cup, 3"h; Saucer, 5½"d, Mark 9 "Ribbon" form.

Plate 135. Cup, 2"h; Saucer, 5½"d, Mark 12, "Ranson" form, large pink floral decor in center of saucer.

Plate 136. Demi-Tasse Cup, 2½"h; Saucer, 5"d, Mark 12, "Silver" form.

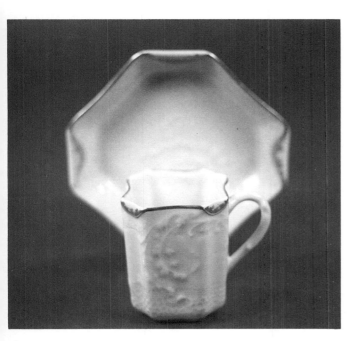

Plate 137. Demi-Tasse Cup, 2½"h; Saucer, 4¼"sq, Mark 6, "Vermicella" form, unusual "Napkin Fold" edge on saucer.

Plate 138. Cup, 2¼"h; Saucer, 5½"d, "Crystal" form, pedestal base, Mark 12 with Mark 13 in gold to denote rich or special decoration.

Plate 139. Cup, 2½"h; Saucer, 5¼"d; Dessert Plate, 7½"d, Mark 34, heavy gold on cobalt blue border.

Plate 140. Demi-Tasse Cup, 2¼"h; Saucer, 4½"d, Mark 9 underglaze and Mark 18 overglaze, "Cannelé" or "Torse" form, hand enamelled.

Plate 141. Unique "Papillon" (Butterfly) Cup, 2½"h, Saucer, 4"d, Mark 6 on cup, Mark 9 on saucer. The butterfly handled pieces are in great demand.

Plate 142. "Papillon" Dessert Service for twelve in original wooden boxes which were designed for Haviland salesmen in the United States. These boxes are extremely rare (see Plate 143). Service consists of twelve demi-tasse cups, 2¼"h; saucers, 4½"d; and dessert plates, 7½"d, Mark 9, rare for complete set in this highly desirable form. (Shanahan Collection)

Plate 143. One of the original cases for "Papillon" dessert service in Plate 142. This case is for the dessert plates, another was for the cups. "HAVILAND & CO., LIMOGES," printed inside top of case with (translated) Gold Medal and Legion of Honor Cross, Paris, 1870, and "Patented U. S. Dec. 16, 1878."

Plate 144. Demi-Tasse Cup, 3"h; Saucer, 5"d, Mark 24, rare "Mont-Mery" mark of Theodore Haviland.

Plate 145. Demi-Tasse Cup, 3"h; Saucer, 5"d, "Ranson" form, gold decor, Mark 11.

Plate 146. Cup, 2½"h; Saucer, 5"d, Mark 7, turquoise border.

Plate 147 Demi-Tasse Cup, 2¼"h; Saucer, 5¼"d, Mark 34, "Boucher" form, deep inside cobalt blue border, heavy gold outer border.

Plate 148. Cup, with Tray 9"l, 6½"w, Mark 11. "Marseille" form. These are usually referred to as Tea and Toast or Sandwich sets.

Plate 149. Egg Cup, Mark 34, 3"h.

Plate 150. Fish Plates, Mark 9, 8½"d, designed by Felix Bracquemond in the *Japonaise* style.

Plate 151. Game Plate, Mark 8, 9"d, "Tresse" or "Basketweave" form, one of a set of six.

Plate 152. Game Plate from set shown in Plate 151.

Plate 153. Ice Cream or Dessert Set, Marks 8 and 9, "Napkin Fold" form, "Old Blackberry" (popular name) pattern: Master Bowl, 9¼"d; Plate, 7"d; Cup, 2"h, Saucer, 5"d, a very popular old pattern.

Plate 154. Invalid Feeder, Mark 12, 2¼"h, 6½"l, undecorated whiteware.

Plate 155. Jam or Marmalade Jar, Mark 12, 4"h, underplate, 6"d, a rather rare tableware item.

Plate 156. Leaf shaped dish, Mark 8 underglaze and Mark 18 overglaze, 5¾"l, 5½"w, fruit decor.

Plate 157. Leaf shaped dish, Mark 9 as an overglaze mark, 8"l, 9¼"w.

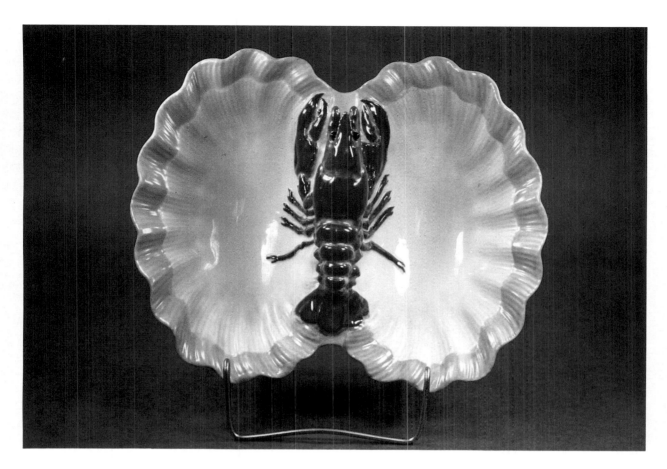

Plate 158. Lobster Dish. Mark 12, 9¼"l, 11½"w, a rare tableware item.

Plate 159. Mayonnaise Dish, leaf shaped, Mark 34, 6½"l, underplate, 7"l.

Plate 160. Menu Stand, Mark 11, 6½″h, 4″w, ''Marseille'' form, unglazed front, sides and back glazed, rare. (Shanahan Collection)

Plate 161. Back of Menu Stand in Plate 160.

Plate 163. Mustache Tea Cup, 2¼"h, Saucer, 6"d, Mark 12.

Plate 162. Mustache Cup, 3"h, Saucer, 6"d, Mark 9, "Marseille" form.

Plate 164. Mustache Cup, 3¼"h, Saucer, 6"d, Mark 7 underglaze and Mark 17 overglaze, gold trim.

Plate 165 Mustard Pot with Underplate, Mark 25, "St. Cloud" form.

Plate 166. Mustard Pot, 2¼"h with ladle, Mark 34.

Plate 167. Mustard Pot, 3¼"h, 4"l, with Underplate, 4½"l, "Marseille" form Mark 11.

Plate 168. Mustard Pot, 2¾"h, 4"w, with Underplate, 4½"l, Mark 11, "Ranson" form.

Plate 169. Oyster Plate, Mark 11, 8½"d, undecorated center, cobalt blue, gold trim.

Plate 170. Oyster Plate, Mark 8, 9″d, different form of marine life in each section.

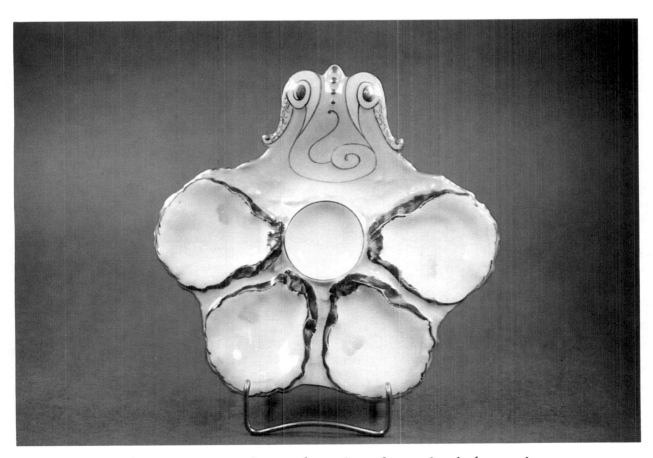

Plate 171. Oyster Plate, 9″d, Mark 8, factory hand decorated.

99

Plate 172. Oyster Plate, Mark 10, 8½"d, "Torse" or "Cannelé" form, cobalt blue background with gold decor.

Plate 173. Oyster Plate. Mark 25, 8½"c. unusual design.

Plate 174. Oyster Plate. Mark 10. floral decor.

Plate 175. Oyster Plate, Mark 9, 8½"d, included separate section for lemon and another for sauce.

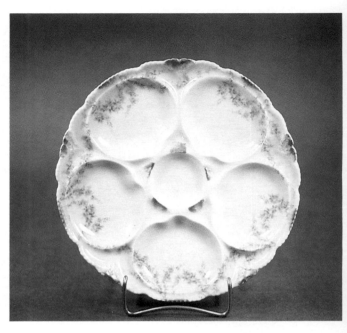

Plate 176. Oyster Plate, Mark 32, 9"d, pink rose garland border.

Plate 177. Pancake Dish, Mark 34, 10½"d, "Rouen" form.

Plate 178. Pitcher, Mark 12, 8¼"h, large pink and red floral decoration.

Plate 179. Pitcher, Mark 11, 9"h, "Ranson" shape, unusual scenic decor with water and trees.

Plate 180. Pitcher, Mark 12, "Portia" form.

Plate 181. Plate, Mark 9, 8½"d, "Diana" shape, matte finish, cream and blue decor.

Plate 182. Plate, Mark 11 underglaze, 8½"d, "Diana" form, special "Feu de Four" (fired longer) decoration (see Mark 14, oveglaze).

Plate 183. Plate, Mark 34, 8½"d.

Plate 184. Plate, Mark 12, 8½″d, "Ranson" shape, "Baltimore Rose" (popular name) pattern in pink.

Plate 185. Plate, Mark 12, 8¾"d, hand enamelled, factory decorated, artist signed "M. Naudin."

Plate 186. Plate, Mark 11, 9"d, pierced border, ornate gold trim.

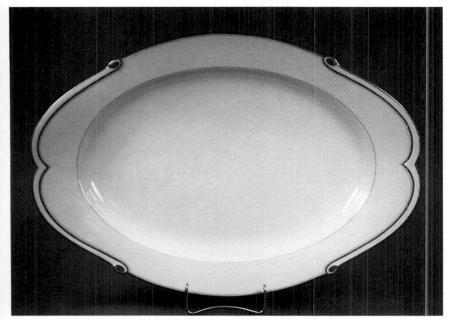

Plate 187. Platter, Mark 16, "Red Edge" decor.

Plate 188. Pudding Set on Charger, 13"d, Mark 12, Serving bowl with liner, "Ranson" form.

Plate 189. Pudding Dish with handled baking dish liner, Mark 34.

Plate 190. Punch or Champagne Cup, Mark 34, 3¼″h, "Satsuma" shape.

Plate 191. Punch or Champagne Cup, Mark 12, "Ranson" form.

Plate 192. Ramekin, Mark 12, 1½″h, 3½″d, Saucer, 5½″d, "Star" form.

Plate 193. Ramekin, Mark 12, 1″h, 3½″d, Saucer, 4¼″d, "Silver" form.

108

Plate 194. Ramekin, Mark 33, 1½"h, 4"d; Saucer, 5"d, "Fantaisie" form, cobalt blue with gold border. These are for baking and serving a particular dish of bread crumbs, eggs and cheese, though they could be used for other dishes as well.

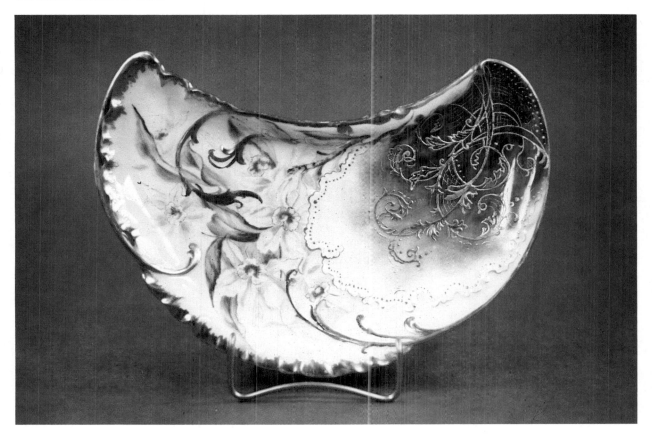

Plate 195. Salad Plate, Mark 11, 10"l, 5½"w, made to fit to side of dinner plate, factory handpainted, "Marseille" shape.

Plate 196. Salad Bowl, Mark 32 (with Theodore abbreviated), 4½″h, 11″d, "Rouen" form (see Plate 197 for matching plates for service). (Shanahan Collection)

Plate 197. Salad Plate, 9″d, one of twelve, matching Salad Bowl in Plate 196 and Tureen in Plate 220.

Plate 198. Individual Salt, Mark 12, 5/8″h, 2″d, "Ranson" form, "The Norma" pattern.

Plate 199. Individual Salt, Mark 12, 2¼″d, "Ranson" form, "Baltimore Rose" (popular name) pattern.

Plate 200. Individual Salt, Mark 12, 2″d, "Derby" form, yellow floral and geometric decor.

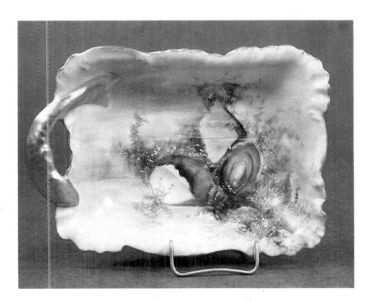

Plate 201. Sardine Box, Mark 11, 6″l, 4½″w, 1¼″h, hand-painted (not factory decorated), unusual item with molded fish handle.

Plate 202. Soup Plate, Mark 32, 9½"d, set of twelve.

Plate 203. Soup Plate, Mark 12, 10"d, unusual scenic Oriental decor.

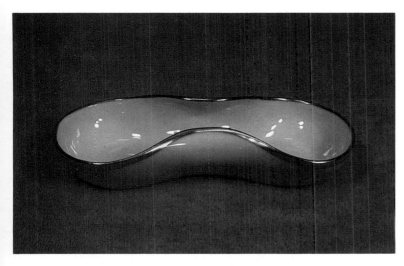

Plate 204. Spoon Tray, Mark 34, 7″l, 3¼″w.

Plate 205. Sugar Bowl, Mark 9, 7″h, rose finial.

Plate 206. Syrup Jug, Mark 34, 4¾″h.

Plate 207. Tea Caddy, Mark 11, 5½″h, "Ranson" form, very scarce item.

Plate 208. Individual Tea Pot, Mark 34, 5½″h.

Plate 209. Tea Pot, Mark 11, 7″h, "Ranson" shape.

Plate 210. Tea Pot, Mark 29, 7½″h, "Pilgrim" form, "Miami" pattern, note angular Art Deco shape.

Plate 211. Tea Pot, Mark 9, 8″h, "Henry II" form.

Plate 212. Tea Pot, Mark 11, 7″h.

Plate 213. Tea Pot, Mark 11, 8″h, "Chantilly" shape.

116

Plate 214. Tea Set. Mark 12, yellow decor with gold and black trim.

Plate 215. Individual Breakfast Tea pot. 5"h, with cup 1½"h, 2"d, Mark 34, "Chelsea" form.

Plate 216. Tea Pot, 6″h, Mark 11, "Ribbon" form.

Plate 217. Tea Pot, Mark 12, 5″h, green ivy with pink flowers.

Plate 218. Tray, Mark 13 overglaze, 15¾"l, 10¾"w, popular "Drop Rose" pattern (popular name) in white, rare in this color. (Shanahan Collection)

Plate 219. Clam Chowder Tureen, Mark 9, 7½"h, 13½"l, 8¼"w, shell finial and handles. "Napkin Fold" form.

Plate 220. Tureen, Mark 32, 8½″h, 14″l, 9½″w, "Rouen" form, part of set (see Plates 196 and 197 for matching pieces).

Plate 221. Tureen, Mark 11, 9″h, 12″l, "Marseille" form.

Plate 222. Covered Vegetable Dish, Mark 9, 7"h, 10½"w, vegetable shaped finial.

Plate 223. Sauce Tureen, Mark 8, 6½"h, 7"w, with underplate, 8"d, "Cable" form, factory handpainted.

Bibliography

d'Albis, Jean and Céleste Romanet. *La Porcelaine de Limoges.* Paris: Editions Sous le Vent, 1980.

Boger, Louise Ade. *The Dictionary of World Pottery and Porcelain.* New York: Charles Scribner's Sons, 1971.

Brunhammer, Yvonne, et al. *Art Nouveau Belgium France: Catalog of an Exhibition Organized by the Institute for the Arts, Rice University, and the Art Institute of Chicago.* Rice University: Institute for the Arts, 1976.

Céramique Impressionniste: L'Atelier Haviland De Paris-Auteuil 1873-1882. Paris: Ancien Hotel Des Archevêques De Sens; Décembre 1974, Février 1975.

Collard, Elizabeth. *Nineteenth-Century Pottery and Porcelain in Canada.* Montreal: McGill University Press, 1967.

Cushion, J.P. *Pocket Book of German Ceramic Marks:* London, Faber and Faber, 1961.

Cushion, J.P. *Pocket Book of French and Italian Ceramic Marks.* London: Faber & Faber, 1965.

Gaston, Mary Frank. *The Collector's Encyclopedia of Limoges Porcelain.* Paducah, Kentucky: Collector Books, 1980.

Jacobsen, Gertrude Tatnall. *Haviland China: Volume One.* Des Moines, Iowa: Wallace-Homestead, 1979.

Klapthor, Margaret Brown. *White House China.* Washington, D.C.: Smithsonian Institution Press, 1975.

Kovel Ralph M. and Terry H. Kovel. *Dictionary of Marks: Pottery and Porcelain.* New York: Crown Publishers, Inc., 1972.

Lesur, Adrien and Tardy. *Les Porcelaines Francaises.* Paris: Tardy, 1967.

"Limoges ou Deux Siecles de Porcelaine." Pp. 87-103 in *Revue des Industries d'art Offrir.* August, 1978.

McClinton, Katharine Morrison. *Art Deco A Guide For Collectors.* New York: Clarkson N. Potter, Inc. 1972.

Mésière, Ernest (ed.). *Porcelaine Theodore Haviland.* Paris: Haviland Company, 1912.

Schleiger, Arlene. *Two Hundred Patterns of Haviland China, Book I.* Omaha, Nebraska: Arlene Schleiger, Fourth Revised Edition, 1973.

Simodynes, Carolyn and Edward Simodynes. "Haviland Art Pottery Part I: Faience," *The Antique Trader,* March 16, 1983a.

Simodynes, Carolyn and Edward Simodynes. "Haviland Art Pottery Part 2: Stoneware," *The Antique Trader.* March 30, 1983b.

Tilmans, Emile. *Porcelaines De France.* Paris: Editions Mondes, 1953.

Wood, Serry. *Haviland Limoges.* Watkins-Glen, New York: Century House, 1951.

Young, Harriet. *Grandmother's Haviland.* Second Revised Edition. Des Moines, Iowa: Wallace-Homestead Book Co., 170.

Object Index

Price Guide

Plate 1. Coffee Pot $400.00-450.00
Plate 2. Vase, pair $2,500.00-3,000.00
Plate 3. Matching vase to Plate 2
Plate 4. Elephant Humidor $10,000.00-12,000.00
Plate 5. Vase $1,200.00-1,400.00
Plate 6. Teapot $65.00-70.00
Plate 7. Water Pitcher $125.00-140.00
Plate 8. Coffee Pot $65.00-70.00
Plate 9. Coffee Pot $65.00-70.00
Plate 10, 11, 12. Complete dinner service for
    six in this design $2,500.00-3,000.00
Plate 13. Complete dinner service for
    six with accessories in this design $700.00-800.00
Plate 14. Sugar $60.00-70.00
    Teapot $75.00-85.00
Plate 15. Creamer & Sugar, set $145.00-165.00
Plate 16. Footbath $500.00-650.00
Plate 17. Footbath from Plate 16
Plate 18. Pitcher $75.00-85.00
Plate 19. Creamer $45.00-50.00
Plate 20. Mouth Rinse Ewer $140.00-155.00
Plate 21. Covered Vegetable $110.00-115.00
Plate 22. Cake Plate $65.00-75.00
Plate 23. Cuspidor $150.00-175.00
Plate 24 and 25. Wash Set and accessories,
    complete set $800.00-900.00
Plate 26. Terra Cotta Gourd Vase $800.00-1,000.00
Plate 27. Back view of Plate 26
Plate 28. Terra Cotta Jug Vase $1,500.00-1,800.00
Plate 29. Terra Cotta Jardiniere $1,500.00-1,800.00
Plate 30. Terra Cotta Vases, pair $900.00-1,200.00
Plate 31. Terra Cotta Vase $400.00-500.00
Plate 32. Back view of Plate 31
Plate 33. Terra Cotta Vase $400.00-500.00
Plate 34. Stoneware Jug $800.00-900.00
Plate 35. Terra Cotta Vase $2,000.00-2,500.00
Plate 36. Vase $3,000.00-3,500.00
Plates 37-43. Napoleon Bonaparte and his
    Ladies, set $2,600.00-3,000.00
Plate 44. Miniature Tea Set $250.00-350.00
Plate 45. Miniature Chocolate Pot $85.00-100.00
Plate 46. Miniature Chocolate Pot $75.00-85.00
Plate 47. Salesman's Sample Chocolate
    Pot $110.00-125.00
Plate 48. Salesman's Sample Cup
    and Saucer $80.00-100.00
Plate 49. Aurene Glass $250.00-300.00
Plate 50. Oyster Plate, each $600.00-800.00
Plate 51. Collector Plate $150.00-175.00
Plate 52. Railroad China, Ice Cream Shell $100.00-115.00
Plate 53. Railroad China, Platter $100.00-115.00
Plate 54. Railroad China, Platter $350.00-400.00
Plate 55. Railroad China, Cup and Saucer $125.00-150.00
Plate 56. Club Ware Handled Egg Cup
    and Saucer $45.00-55.00
Plate 57. Commemorative Plate $110.00-125.00
Plate 58. Hotel China Salad Plate $75.00-85.00
Plate 59. Hotel China Plate $100.00-115.00

Plate 60. Hotel China Spooner $125.00-150.00
Plate 61. Advertising China Ash Tray $45.00-50.00
Plate 62. Sandoz Monkey Tobacco Jar ... $600.00-700.00
Plate 63. Sandoz Duck Pitcher $500.00-600.00
Plate 64. Sandoz Fishes Knife Rest $275.00-325.00
Plate 65. Sandoz Creamer $300.00-400.00
    Coffee Pot $400.00-500.00
Plate 66. Sandoz Pequin Tea Pot $450.00-550.00
Plate 67. Cavalier Bust $4,000.00-5,000.00
Plate 68. Back view of Plate 67
Plate 69. Basket $95.00-100.00
Plate 70. Bon-Bon Basket $125.00-150.00
Plate 71. Chamberstick $125.00-150.00
Plate 72. Basket $120.00-140.00
Plate 73. Liquor Decanter $75.00-95.00
Plate 74. Match Box $65.00-75.00
Plate 75. Ferner with liner $225.00-275.00
Plate 76. Candlestick $100.00-120.00
Plate 77. Vase $1,000.00-1,200.00
Plate 78. Powder Box $135.00-150.00
Plate 79. Hair Receiver $135.00-150.00
Plate 80. Shaving Mug $85.00-100.00
Plate 81. Ring Tree $75.00-85.00
Plate 82. Vase $175.00-225.00
Plate 83. Back view of Plate 82
Plate 84. Vase $175.00-225.00
Plate 85. Back view of Plate 84
Plate 86. Vase $225.00-275.00
Plate 87. Vase $75.00-100.00
Plate 88. Vase $175.00-225.00
Plate 89. Vase $800.00-1,000.00
Plate 90. Jardiniere $145.00-165.00
Plate 91. Jardiniere $165.00-185.00
Plate 92. Ormulu Mounted Compote $100.00-125.00
Plate 93. Same as Plate 92
Plate 94. Berry Set, set $350.00-400.00
Plate 95. Bon-Bon Plate $95.00-110.00
Plate 96. Covered Bouillon $95.00-110.00
Plate 97. Covered Bouillon $85.00-100.00
Plate 98. Butter Pats, each $15.00-20.00
Plate 99. Butter Tub $75.00-85.00
Plate 100. Cake Plate $150.00-175.00
Plate 101. Cake Stand $85.00-95.00
Plate 102. Chocolate Pot $200.00-250.00
Plate 103. Chocolate Pot $150.00-175.00
Plate 104. Chocolate Pot $150.00-175.00
Plate 105. Chocolate Pot $150.00-175.00
Plate 106. Chocolate Pot $450.00-500.00
Plate 107. Chocolate Pot $150.00-175.00
Plate 108. Chocolate Pot $70.00-90.00
Plate 109. Chocolate Pot $150.00-175.00
Plate 110. Chocolate Set $700.00-900.00
Plate 111. Chocolate Set $2,500.00-3,000.00
Plate 112. Chocolate Pot $150.00-175.00
Plate 113. Chocolate Pot $225.00-275.00
Plate 114. Chocolate Pot $150.00-175.00
Plate 115. Claret Jug $110.00-130.00

Plate 116. Milk Pitcher $120.00-140.00
         Coffee Pot $165.00-190.00
Plate 117. Coffee Pot $150.00-175.00
Plate 118. Coffee Pot $150.00-175.00
Plate 119. Coffee Pot $150.00-175.00
Plate 120. Coffee Pot $150.00-175.00
Plate 121. Compote $125.00-135.00
Plate 122. Compote $200.00-250.00
Plate 123. Compote $350.00-400.00
Plate 124. Compote $160.00-175.00
Plate 125. Cracker Jar $110.00-125.00
Plate 126. Cracker Jar $145.00-160.00
Plate 127. Cracker Jar $160.00-180.00
Plate 128. Creamer $135.00-155.00
Plate 129. Creamer & Sugar, set $125.00-150.00
Plate 130. Dessert Creamer & Sugar $140.00-160.00
Plate 131. Demi-Tasse Cup and Saucer . . . $45.00-55.00
Plate 132. Demi-Tasse Cup and Saucer . . . $45.00-55.00
Plate 133. Demi-Tasse Cup and Saucer . . . $45.00-55.00
Plate 134. Demi-Tasse Cup and Saucer . . . $45.00-55.00
Plate 135. Cup and Saucer $75.00-85.00
Plate 136. Demi-Tasse Cup and Saucer . . . $45.00-55.00
Plate 137. Demi-Tasse Cup and Saucer . . . $80.00-100.00
Plate 138. Cup and Saucer $80.00-100.00
Plate 139. Cup, Saucer and Dessert Plate,
         set $150.00-175.00
Plate 140. Demi-Tasse Cup and Saucer . . . $80.00-100.00
Plate 141. "Papillon" Cup and Saucer . . . $100.00-125.00
Plate 142 and 143. "Papillon" Dessert Service for
         Twelve with wood boxes $2,200.00-2,500.00
Plate 144. Demi-Tasse Cup and Saucer . . . $60.00-80.00
Plate 145. Demi-Tasse Cup and Saucer . . . $45.00-55.00
Plate 146. Cup and Saucer $40.00-50.00
Plate 147. Demi-Tasse Cup and Saucer . . . $90.00-100.00
Plate 148. Cup with Tray $60.00-70.00
Plate 149. Egg Cup $45.00-55.00
Plate 150. Fish Plates, pair $150.00-175.00
Plate 151. Game Plate $45.00-55.00
Plate 152. Game Plate $45.00-55.00
Plate 153. Ice Cream or Dessert Set,
         set for 4 . . . . $450.00-500.00
Plate 154. Invalid Feeder $50.00-55.00
Plate 155. Jam or Marmalade Jar $145.00-160.00
Plate 156. Leaf-shaped Dish, pair $100.00-125.00
Plate 157. Leaf-shaped Dish $60.00-70.00
Plate 158. Lobster Dish $225.00-275.00
Plate 159. Mayonnaise Dish $75.00-85.00
Plate 160, 161. Menu Stand $165.00-190.00
Plate 162. Mustache Cup and Saucer $125.00-135.00
Plate 163. Mustache Tea Cup and Saucer $150.00-160.00
Plate 164. Mustache Cup and Saucer $135.00-150.00
Plate 165. Mustard Pot with Underplate . . $90.00-100.00
Plate 166. Mustard Pot with Ladle $60.00-70.00
Plate 167. Mustard Pot with Underplate . $110.00-120.00
Plate 168. Mustard Pot with Underplate . $110.00-120.00
Plate 169. Oyster Plate $85.00-100.00

Plate 170. Oyster Plate $80.00-90.00
Plate 171. Oyster Plate $100.00-115.00
Plate 172. Oyster Plate $85.00-100.00
Plate 173. Oyster Plate $110.00-125.00
Plate 174. Oyster Plate $80.00-95.00
Plate 175. Oyster Plate $90.00-100.00
Plate 176. Oyster Plate $90.00-100.00
Plate 177. Pancake Dish $100.00-125.00
Plate 178. Pitcher $200.00-225.00
Plate 179. Pitcher $165.00-185.00
Plate 180. Pitcher $150.00-165.00
Plate 181. Plate $30.00-35.00
Plate 182. Plate $50.00-60.00
Plate 183. Plate $30.00-35.00
Plate 184. Plate $50.00-65.00
Plate 185. Plate $50.00-65.00
Plate 186. Plate $95.00-110.00
Plate 187. Platter $75.00-100.00
Plate 188. Pudding Set on Charger, Serving Bowl
         with Liner, set $175.00-225.00
Plate 189. Pudding Dish with liner $150.00-175.00
Plate 190. Punch or Champagne Cup $70.00-80.00
Plate 191. Punch or Champagne Cup $75.00-85.00
Plate 192. Ramekin and Saucer $40.00-50.00
Plate 193. Ramekin and Saucer $40.00-50.00
Plate 194. Ramekin and Saucer $90.00-100.00
Plate 195. Salad Plate $80.00-90.00
Plate 196 and 197. Salad Bowl
         and Plates $1,800.00-2,000.00
Plate 198. Individual Salt $30.00-35.00
Plate 199. Individual Salt $90.00-100.00
Plate 200. Individual Salt $35.00-40.00
Plate 201. Sardine Box $80.00-100.00
Plate 202. Soup Plate, set of 12 . . . . . . $1,500.00-1,600.00
Plate 203. Soup Plate, each $65.00-75.00
Plate 204. Spoon Tray $65.00-75.00
Plate 205. Sugar Bowl $65.00-75.00
Plate 206. Syrup Jug $90.00-100.00
Plate 207. Tea Caddy $125.00-145.00
Plate 208. Individual Tea Pot $80.00-90.00
Plate 209. Tea Pot $140.00-160.00
Plate 210. Tea Pot $75.00-100.00
Plate 211. Tea Pot $140.00-160.00
Plate 212. Tea Pot $125.00-145.00
Plate 213. Tea Pot $140.00-160.00
Plate 214. Tea Set $150.00-175.00
Plate 215. Individual Breakfast Tea Pot
         and Cup $95.00-110.00
Plate 216. Tea Pot $95.00-110.00
Plate 217. Tea Pot $65.00-75.00
Plate 218. Tray $450.00-500.00
Plate 219. Clam Chowder Tureen $150.00-200.00
Plate 220. Tureen $350.00-450.00
Plate 221. Tureen $225.00-275.00
Plate 222. Covered Vegetable Dish $140.00-160.00
Plate 223. Sauce Tureen $200.00-250.00